SAINT BENEDICT JOSEPH LABRE

Saint Benedict Joseph Labre
Votary of Holy Poverty and Pilgrim

by
C. L. WHITE

CANA PRESS

Originally published in 1906
by Burns & Oates, London.

Newly typeset and edited by Notre Dame Priory
Cana Press © 2025, all rights reserved.
No part of this book may be reproduced or transmitted, in
any form or by any means, without permission.

For information, address:
PO Box 85,
Colebrook,
Tasmania, 7027,
Australia
info@canapress.com.au
www.canapress.com.au
notredamemonastery.org

ISBN
978-0-6454653-9-6

FOREWORD

In preparing this sketch of the life of Saint Benedict Labre, I am indebted chiefly to the research of French historians for dates and facts concerning him.

Saint Benedict Joseph Labre was born at Amettes, Pas de Calais, 1748.

Died at Rome in the odour of sanctity, 1783.

Proclaimed Venerable by Pius IX, 1859.

Canonized by Leo XIII, December 8th, 1881.

Saint Benedict Joseph Labre's Feast is kept on the anniversary of the day of his death, April 16th.

C. L. White

CONTENTS

Foreword. v
Birth and Childhood of Benedict Joseph 1
Benedict Joseph's First Communion 7
Benedict Returns to Amettes 15
Benedict goes to 21
Notre Dame de la Trappe at Mortagne 21
Eighty Miles Farther to the Abbey of Sept-Fonts 27
His First Visit to Loretto 33
Benedict's Discourse. 39
From Loretto, along the Adriatic Coast, and Naples 43
Benedict is Threatened with Imprisonment as a Vagrant. . . 49
Prison, and the Crown of Thorns. 53
Life in Rome 59
He Receives 65
Admiration and Indignity with Equal Unconcern. 65
Distant Pilgrimages and Fourth Return to Rome 73
What some Persons said of him. 79
A Priest Observes him as an Example 85
His Last Pilgrimage to Loretto. 89

'I have just Given Communion to a Saint'. 93
The Saint's one deep Grief is the
       Ingratitude of Men towards Jesus Christ 99
'The Crown of Life' 103
Prayers 113

BIRTH AND CHILDHOOD OF BENEDICT JOSEPH

On the 26th day of March in the year 1748, there was a deep but subdued joy in the home of Jean-Baptiste Labre; for to him and his wife Anne-Barbe Grandsir was born their first child—a boy. The parents belonged to the simple, dignified and independent class of French small proprietors. Their dwelling was in the pretty, sheltered village of Amettes, then in the diocese of Boulogne, now in that of Arras. They cultivated their own patrimony, and were notable for their great piety.

The custom of hearing holy Mass every day was traditional, and one member of the family always bore the name of Joseph, showing that the guardian of the Blessed Virgin and her Divine Son, was invoked as protector of the Labre family life. Jean-Baptiste and his wife welcomed their first-born with tender thanksgiving.

From his devout mother's heart went up a prayer that a vocation for the priesthood might be given to him. She could never have imagined the extraordinary vocation her fair child would receive from the inspiration of God!

The infant was baptized on the day after his birth by his uncle and Godfather, Francis Joseph Labre, Vicar of Ames, and later curé of Erin. The babe received at the font the names Benedict Joseph. He responded to his mother's care of soul and body by his quick intelligence and docility. From her he soon learned the first elements of piety, his baby hand making the sign of the Cross with sweetest reverence; the first words he lisped were the names of Jesus and Mary. He loved to be taken to the church, his mother said she was able to keep him with her there as long as she liked; in no place was he more peaceful and happy, showing none of the ordinary restlessness of childhood. With the dawn of reason he seemed to realise the presence of God, and never to lose a sense of it. In a spirit of love and reverence he soon began to have a horror of anything that could offend God. This feeling impressed him so deeply that it kept him apart from the usual amusements of children, for fear lest his natural impetuosity might lead him into some outbreak of temper. So early did he begin that mastery over himself which was later to make him a model of heroic virtue. At the early age of five years he began to practise self-denial, and check the love of earthly things. He had the benefit of his parents' good example and their careful training; but special grace enlightened him, so quickly did the boy grasp the principles of the Gospel: so readily did he understand the obligation to serve God, to take up the Cross and follow Jesus Christ in the difficult path of self-sacrifice.

Benedict Joseph already showed a great attraction to prayer; this grew daily stronger when he went to pass the greater part of his fifth year under the roof of his maternal grandmother, Anne Theodore Vincent, whose home was also in the village of Amettes. Here his precocity of mind and his admirable qualities became more and more apparent. Jacque Joseph Vincent, another of his uncles, was at this time studying for the priesthood. He noticed his little nephew's great aptitude for piety, and devoted part of his own time to the child, teaching him to read, so that he might learn the catechism and other devotional books. This uncle's care and influence helped to form Benedict Joseph's character. The boy watched his uncle, obeyed him readily, and took his reprimands with gentleness and humility.

A year later, when this uncle entered the seminary to prepare to take Orders, Benedict Joseph's parents brought him home, so that during the winter he might attend the village school which was nearer to their house. After a short time with the beginners, he passed under the instruction of the school director and Vicar of the parish, M. l'Abbé d' Hanotel, who soon saw that this was no ordinary child. His modesty, sweetness, his piety and tranquility were remarkable. He seemed to have none of the usual faults of children of his age. One of his masters said: 'Amongst the two thousand pupils I have governed, not one has possessed such excellent qualities'. Another wished to test him by repeated reproaches and severity, but the boy received these trials in perfect humility, and only made greater efforts in self-conquest, giving ever more diligence and application, especially in regard to religious instruction. He was respectful and obedient to all in authority over him, gentle and patient to his comrades, always bright and contented.

The secret of this was his abiding sense of God's presence; all his actions were done to please the supreme Majesty, whose power and goodness were so vividly imprinted upon his young mind.

He was taught by his parents to go to Confession when he was six years old. As soon as he was able to serve Mass, this was the great joy of the day to him. The love of prayer grew so strong, that instead of joining in games at recreation time, he would go away quietly into the church to pray, or sit apart reading his books of devotion. And this he did without offending the other children, who generally loved him; some looked upon him as a model and tried to follow his example. His humility disarmed envy, and his presence acted as a check upon disorder.

At the age of ten he was sent to the school at Nédon, a degree higher than that of Amettes. Masters and school-fellows soon began to find out his merits. The boy kept his conscience so clear and tranquil that M. Delrue, the principal, wrote later: 'The satisfaction that this child gave me was so complete that I do not remember ever to have had occasion to say to him a single word that would give him pain.'

Benedict Joseph's conduct at home was no less admirable, he obeyed the least wish of father or mother with ready cheerfulness; and they daily thanked God for the gift of so good a son.

There was plenty of scope for self-denial and amiability in the large family of little children—Benedict was the eldest of fifteen. He taught his brothers and sisters, comforted them in their small troubles, and edified them by his constant kindness and patience. About this time he began his secret practice of mortification, refusing a number of trifles that give pleasure to the young. His mother found him one evening out of his bed, lying upon the floor, where he meant to sleep. When she remonstrated, he said it was to harden himself.

It must not be supposed that he attained this degree of self-command without effort. On the contrary, he had to fight valiantly against his natural impetuosity, and other temptations of his age, thoughtlessness, inattention, impatience, greediness, idleness. He had an especial horror for the sin of detraction and would not go near those who were likely to speak evil of their neighbours. Any breach of charity made him miserable, and in the different houses where he was welcomed, he would read aloud some edifying book to put a stop to useless or idle gossip.

When he served Mass, villagers who were present would say to each other afterwards, 'Benedict Joseph is like an angel.' His attitude of rapt devotion, his azure blue eyes, and fair abundant hair made others declare he had a *tête de cherubin* [i.e. the face of an angel].

In the year 1753 Perpetual Adoration was established in the diocese. When the Forty Hours Exposition took place at Amettes, the child scarcely left the Church. He saw death for the first time when his little sister aged a few months was taken. Benedict remained gazing at her with reverence, as he thought of her in Heaven.

'Ah, baby,' he exclaimed 'how you are to be envied! O that I could have the same happiness!'

BENEDICT JOSEPH'S FIRST COMMUNION

He made it at the age of twelve. His uncle and Godfather, M. Labre, curé of Erin in 1752, came over to Amettes to see his brother, and was so much struck by the good dispositions of his godchild, that he proposed to the parents that Benedict Joseph should return with him to Erin to be prepared for his first Communion, and to learn Latin in readiness for the ecclesiastical state. After some hesitation—for the boy was very dear to his parents, and now most useful to them in helping to bring up the other children—they yielded.

Then began that love and veneration for Jesus in the Blessed Sacrament which was to gather intensity day by day. The sublime truths of the Gospel, the death and passion of our Lord, His love for man in deigning to remain with them in the Holy Eucharist, took hold of the boys imagination, and filled his heart, to the gradual, and almost complete exclusion of every other object. His soul vibrated between a deep sense of his own unworthiness to be united to Jesus, and the ardent longing to receive Him. Above all was a thirst to make all the reparation he could for the slights, irreverences, the coldness and ingratitude of men towards the divine Victim.

After the most minute examination of his conscience, he excited himself to contrition by dwelling upon the sufferings of our Saviour for our sins; he then made a general Confession, and remained in a state of constant recollection. The 4th of September, 1761, was the day of holy joy; it is not easy to describe the feelings of the young saint when he received his God. He seemed to be lifted out of earth, and to be living with the Angels. From that moment he gave himself to the supernatural life without reserve, and the Sacrament of Confirmation, administered by the Bishop of Boulogne on the same day, put the seal of the Holy Spirit upon his resolve.

The effect of Holy Communion on his soul was a great increase of fervour, and to give him a more complete distaste for the world. He shunned all usual fêtes and amusements; they were to him an utter waste of time; the precious time given, he said, to prepare for an eternity in Heaven.

He rose very early, winter and summer; after vocal prayers came meditation: his delight was to serve both the curé's and vicar's masses. The study of Latin made him happy because it is the language of the Church and of her offices. He learned it quickly and with zeal, as also other necessary subjects; but he gave every spare moment to prayer and meditation, visiting the Blessed Sacrament several times during the day.

His holidays were spent in visits to the sick and the poor, who could always be sure of his charity. He would reserve more than half of his own food to give them, as well as alms from the presbytery.

On Sundays after Mass he would often join the groups standing in the square outside the church, and take an opportunity of saying some good words. His presence was a check upon foolish or frivolous talk, and he was so humble, so engaging, that he was welcomed everywhere. People were glad to listen to his speech, or to hear him read.

In three years he had made great progress in knowledge of Latin, history, etc. He could never overcome his distaste for pagan authors. Cicero and Virgil disturbed the calm serenity of his soul, which delighted only in holy Scripture, the lives of the Saints and ascetic books. Those of Père Lejeune, of the Oratory, made an indelible impression on his mind. The sermons on 'The pains of Hell,' and upon 'The small number of the Elect' may be said to have guided his life. He loved to read and meditate the works of Père Louis de Grenade, feeling himself drawn more and more to the absolute practice of Christian virtues and to the penitential life.

As a little child he was happy when alone with God. At the age of sixteen the attraction was so strong that it absorbed him entirely. He no longer cared to gain general knowledge. He still read with eagerness; even when out for the usual walk with his uncle he would take a book so as not to lose time, should the curé pay a visit, or be detained on the road by a parishioner; but works on religion alone occupied him. His mind soared beyond the material world. His one desire was to converse with God, this was the cause of his love for what his friends called solitude. Benedict was never less alone. Shut within a little room rarely used by others of the household, he spent long hours wrapt in contemplation. He came forth imbued with humility, with a tender love of mankind, the souls for whom Christ died; but with an ever increasing distaste for the world and its paltry joys.

Companions of his own age would beg him to join them in their recreations, and holiday excursions, for, despite his gravity, he was a general favourite. Vexed by his refusals, they would try to move him by taunts and reproaches. With gentle calm he would assure them that he was far happier in his little room.

In obedience to his uncle he would sometimes go with companions to the village fêtes, brightly and cheerfully, but soon after his arrival on the scene, he would leave the throng to seek a quiet nook where he could pour out his soul in prayer at the foot of the Cross. Visits to Our Lord in the Blessed Sacrament were the joys of his life, he would walk any distance to attend the Forty Hours' Adoration.

At the age of sixteen he had resolved to find out in which of the religious Orders he 'could reach the highest perfection under the most austere rule.'

He decided upon 'la Trappe'.

He was confirmed in this choice by hearing the curé of a neighbouring parish describe, with enthusiasm, many details of the rule in the Monastery of Notre Dame de la Trappe, at Mortagne, which this Priest had visited. Benedict was never weary of the theme; he managed to gain considerable knowledge of the life of the Trappists, and he began to practise many of their austerities in readiness for the cloister, which was now his sole desire.

He spoke of it to his confessor and director, whose sanction guided him in everything. 'I shall never live in the world,' Benedict said, 'my vocation is to retire into the desert.' His director told him to lay the case at once before his uncle, the curé of Erin. The curé had noticed for some time past that his nephew no longer appeared eager to study; he was docile and obedient, but his heart was not in his work. The curé began to fear that his own cherished hopes of seeing Benedict's great and good qualities turned to account in the priesthood, might after all not be realised. He spoke seriously to him on the subject, urging him to put more energy into the studies which would be so necessary to him as a Priest.

'I must tell you, dear Godfather,' Benedict answered respectfully, 'that I have taken an extreme dislike for all knowledge that does not concern the salvation of my soul. I have tried to overcome it, in order to please you, but I am conquered by a force stronger than my will. I am resolved to enter the cloister, and have chosen the rule of la Trappe as most suitable.'

The good curé looked the astonishment that he could not hide. The austerities of the Trappist for this gentle serious youth!

'You are not old enough yet to decide upon taking such a step,' he said, with grave concern. Remember that your constitution is delicate. Men, far stronger than you, have failed under the trial. If you knew anything of the rule, you would change your mind about entering the novitiate.'

Benedict's answers proved that his idea was no sudden freak of fancy, it had been the subject of long and deep reflection, it had been thought out with ardent prayers for guidance. He showed himself fully acquainted with details of the rule, and firmly resolved to give up the world.

His uncle was impressed. If this was the will of God in regard to Benedict, he was the last man to attempt to oppose it, he would not take the responsibility of checking such aspirations; nevertheless, he told his nephew that the duty of a son of his age was to return to his parents, tell them of his project and obtain their consent.

Benedict lost no time on the way; four years had passed since he left the paternal roof, but instead of joy, his visit brought consternation into the family group. His father and mother saw all their plans for his future upset, they too feared for his health; they were not convinced that Providence was leading him in that direction, and they used all their eloquence to turn him from his purpose. His mother assured him he could serve God far more efficaciously as a zealous Priest than buried in the cloister. But if he felt the charge of souls in a parish too heavy, he should not be pressed to undertake it. He should enjoy all the advantages of an eldest son in their home, where his aid would be invaluable. Every argument that tenderness could suggest was brought to bear on his resolution, but Benedict was immoveable. His heart was tortured by his parents' grief, yet he besought them not to oppose his vocation. They admired his firmness, and the wisdom of his replies, as well as his patience and gentleness, but they were no less resolved not to yield to his wishes. They pointed out that he owed them obedience, he was not yet of age to be master of his own career, that for the present he must continue his studies at Erin. Their grief was intense; this first-born son was the centre of so many fond hopes. It was the dearest wish of their hearts that he should be a priest, perhaps one day the revered curé of their own village of Amettes; but that he should drop out of their life, to consign himself to an open tomb, where he would be hidden from their sight forever! Impossible, they could not agree to that yet!

Benedict, in obedience, resumed work at Erin, but redoubled his austerities; he led the life of an anchorite, only quitting the presbytery to go to the church. His confessions and communions were more frequent, he was more than ever devoted to prayer. He slept upon planks in coldest weather, and would give his whole dinner away to anyone in need. He was quietly preparing for the life at la Trappe.

The interior voice that called him to leave all things was not silenced, and God permitted him to be severely tried by perplexities of conscience that wrung his soul. This lasted for two years, when an event took place which put his zeal and charity to the test.

In August, 1766, a virulent epidemic broke out in the peaceful village of Erin. The rustic homes were filled with sick and dying, contagion was so swift that the mortality increased each day. The devoted curé was everywhere among the sufferers, his nephew Benedict at his side. Together they lavished care and attentions to the stricken. Benedict took upon himself the most repellent services. He worked hard also in the stables to preserve the animals so precious to their owners.

All too soon the curé was attacked by the malady, and notwithstanding the prayers of his parishioners, and Benedict's tender nursing, he succumbed, giving up his soul to God on the 13th of September, 1776, at the age of fifty-two.

The loss of his wise and kind guardian was a cruel blow to Benedict's grateful heart, but grief only helped to detach him from the world. With thoughts fixed upon God he worked harder than ever among the sick and dying, not a thought did he give to the danger to which his own young life was exposed, nor did he appear to remember that, since his uncle's death, he was no longer in any way bound to this afflicted parish. He left to other members of the family the care of proving succession to the property belonging to the late curé, and he devoted himself to the villagers for six weeks more, until the scourge of typhus had passed. He was so beloved by the parishioners that they saw him go with the greatest regret. 'We hoped,' they said, 'that you might have succeeded your uncle in the parish, and stayed with us as our pastor in his place, had he but lived a few years longer!'

Benedict's reply was that he did not feel himself called to the ministry, and should never dare to take upon himself the care of souls; 'I am not worthy of it,' he added in deep humility.

BENEDICT RETURNS TO AMETTES

Of his inheritance from his uncle he took nothing but the works of Père Lejeune, and came back to his family for the feast of All Saints, November, 1766. He was now nearly nineteen, and expected no further opposition from his parents, to his ardent wish to enter the rule of la Trappe. Good Christians though they were, they still withheld their consent, in the hope that he would be content to serve God in the world as a secular priest.

'I should have to fear damnation,' was his answer, 'if I were to take upon myself to work for the salvation of others in the world, God calls me to solitude.'

'How could you live, dear son,' asked his mother 'if you were to retire into a desert.'

'I should live like the hermits of old, upon herbs, and fruits of the field.'

'But the hermits were men of much stronger type than those of today; besides, God worked miracles for them.'

'Is God any less powerful now? If he wrought miracles then to sustain His servants, He will do so still. Ah! Dear mother, He works unseen miracles every day; yes, believe me, one can do everything with the help of God. To will is to be able, when He is with us.' This was Benedict's answer to all objections. He lived at home as if dead to the world, conforming himself as much as possible to the rule he longed to embrace. His extreme delicacy of conscience showed itself in various little counsels which he gave on different occasions. When his mother had to make some purchases, he gently reminded her that she should not argue too keenly about the price, lest the vendors might be tempted to tell lies.

He invariably slept upon the floor, but disarranged his bed, so that his asceticism might not be noticed. It was not always easy to elude his mother's vigilance. She surprised him on the bare boards, his head upon a log of knotty wood, and she severely rebuked him.

'Do not be angry,' he said. 'If God calls me to la Trappe, I must prepare myself to follow the rule.' This proved to her that his desire was unchanged.

Benedict's parents, however, though fit to send him to Conteville, to live in the house of his maternal uncle, the Abbé Vincent, who was Vicar of the parish. This was the young uncle who had taken so much interest in his nephew when a child. Their tastes were almost identical. Benedict was free to practise austere rules of the religious life. Poverty, silence, obedience, self-denial, asking nothing, and never losing his sweet serenity. His studies were more satisfactory, his progress became marked, he soon excelled in translations of Latin authors. For some time the Abbé Vincent was without a servant, and prepared the meals himself; he rivalled his nephew in the practice of mortification and charity. Sometimes when dinner was ready, he would look at Benedict, reflecting for a moment, then say, 'We are both in good health, would not a piece of bread be enough for us, there are several sick and infirm in the village whose need is greater than ours.' In delight Benedict would carry off the provisions, meat and vegetables, to leave them at the houses indicated. The Vicar's holy charity caused him to distribute even the furniture of his house among his poorer neighbours. The room he occupied had no boarded floor, so to supply the want of chairs the Abbé Vincent dug a large hole, on the rim of which he and his nephew contentedly seated themselves to continue studies in Latin. Where in these days could such a blend of charity, rusticity, and refinement be found!

Benedict was happy in the life at Conteville; he accompanied his uncle to all the religious ceremonies that took place in the neighbourhood; joyfully he would load himself with ornaments to be used to enhance the solemnity: the processional cross, candlesticks, bouquets, etc. He would walk any distance to attend the Forty Hours' devotion, when, absorbed in contemplation, he would remain the whole day upon his knees immoveable.

During Lent, in 1767, a mission was preached in the surrounding villages. Benedict followed all the exercises, and laid his case before the missionaries, telling them of his aspirations and the difficulties he met.

After serious examination they approved of his resolution, and the Abbé Vincent, seeing his nephew's constancy, thought that four years was a sufficient trial of it, and now offered to speak to Benedict's parents himself; advising Benedict to try his vocation with the Carthusian monks, whose monastery was near, rather than go to la Trappe.

This being decided, the Abbé Vincent had less difficulty in persuading his sister that she must no longer oppose so evident a vocation.

After Easter in April, 1767, Benedict set out for the Carthusian monastery of Val-Sainte-Aldegonde in the diocese of Saint Omer. The monks received him with kindness as a guest; he quickly explained the motive of his visit. The religious to whom he spoke, Dom Cyril Piefort, replied that, owing to the temporal affairs of their house, it was impossible to take novices, but he must not be discouraged, nor give up his project; he should apply to another house of their Order, Notre Dame des Prés near Neuville in the diocese of Boulogne.

Benedict obediently went there without loss of time. One of his uncles, Francis Joseph Vincent, Canon of the Church of Our Lady of Wailingcourt, accompanied him. The Canon had come from Cambrai to see his relatives, and was greatly edified by what he saw of Benedict's character. Together they appeared at the monastery gates, having walked every step of the way. The Prior heard his request with great interest, then said, as Benedict was not yet twenty, there was no immediate hurry; he must finish his studies and learn plain-chant and dialectics. The disappointment was very great. Benedict had felt certain of success; he bore it with his usual submission, and returned to Amettes.

His parents, now ready to give their son an opportunity of acquiring the necessary subjects, considered ways and means. He was placed with the Vicar of Ligny-les-Aires. This priest, Joseph Adrian Dufour, had been a pupil of the good curé of Erin, and was glad to show his appreciation to the family.

Benedict was four months in his school; he enjoyed ecclesiastical chant—his ear was correct, his voice singularly sweet and penetrating—but logic made no appeal to his interest.

He made swift and sure progress in the science of the Cross, edifying all who knew him, and, as if he could never hear enough of the sublime truths of his holy Faith, he attended all the Catechism classes at Ligny, although in his twentieth year.

When he thought he knew enough logic to be accepted, he made another attempt. This time the Prior found him sufficiently advanced, and noting his great attraction to the religious life, consented to receive him then and there.

When the gates swung on their hinges and closed behind him, shutting out the world, Benedict thought he had reached his haven.

God tries His Saints in ways unsearchable. The interior light which had shone on the young postulant's path, and made rough places plain, was suddenly withdrawn; Benedict's spirit was plunged in unspeakable desolation. The anxiety he had felt at Erin was as nothing to what he now endured. Isolation, and lack of movement increased his distress; he would have liked manual labour in common, and more severe penances; la Trappe had always been the object of his wishes. Despite his sufferings, he was faithful to the present rule in every particular.

But the good fathers saw that his health would give way. After six weeks they told him that it was evidently not the will of God that he should remain in their institute. In sorrow the poor postulant retraced his steps; one hope was left to him; it was that he might yet be a Trappist.

BENEDICT GOES TO NOTRE DAME DE LA TRAPPE AT MORTAGNE

His parents opened their arms to him, and believed he would sigh no more after the cloister. But the first morning after his arrival he humbly declared that his intention was to follow his first inspiration, which had been given up in deference to their wishes. His family and friends clustered round him beseeching him with tears and prayers to be satisfied with the trial he had made.

His answer was to kneel, with bowed head, for the father's and mother's blessing, as he begged their forgiveness for his faults, and for the grief he caused them.

Having embraced them, he turned and went his way. Sixty miles he travelled on foot, taking neither money nor provisions and exposed to heavy rains. On the 25th of November, 1767, he stood and knocked at the monastery door.

He was told with kindness and sympathy that he was too

young and too frail in health to be admitted into the novitiate. For several days he renewed his request, waiting in the hope of successfully pleading for a more favourable reply. In vain. The inflexible rule admitted no postulant under the age of twenty-four. Further appeal was useless.

In silence he departed, dejection in his heart and in his bearing, as he still 'adored the inscrutable will of God'. That is what he said on reaching home in a pitiable state of physical exhaustion, to be welcomed with joy by his mother.

'This son,' she said, 'had given his parents one grief only, and that was his wish to quit them to enter a monastery.'

She expected now to keep him in the world. His purpose was, however, unshaken; the idea of a delay of four years caused him incessant anxiety and trouble. He continued his life of mortification, as if he were in the cloister, his patience, his charity, his humility were admirable. His severity towards himself distressed his mother.

'Benedict is too hard upon himself,' she would say. 'It is his one defect, if it can be called a defect, and he redeems it by so many other graces.'

In the spirit of obedience he did all that was suggested in the family life, instructing his younger brothers, taking a share in the farm work, but the interior voice was so insistent that he reproached himself for not having been more urgent, more vigorous in his pleading for admission at la Trappe.

After twenty months of fidelity to all his exercises of piety and prayer, seeking ever more earnestly light from Heaven, he heard of a mission given fifteen miles away, near Boulogne. He obtained leave to attend it. There he was advised to take counsel of the Bishop and abide by his decision.

To carry out this purpose Benedict went on to Boulogne; he was cordially received by a friend and relative of his family, Canon

Michael Joseph Flamand. Encouraged by this good priest, he lost no time in asking for an audience. The Bishop felt interested directly, listened to him, questioned him at length, and was touched and edified by the insight he gained into this rare character, so devout, so transparent, and above all, so rich in the grace of humility. After learning all details, the prelate said to him, 'Have confidence, return to the Carthusians at Neuville, and ask for readmission.'

This answer was most unexpected.

But whatever reluctance and difficulty Benedict felt in going back to a place where he had suffered such mental distress and been dismissed, he did not hesitate to accept the order as sent to him from God. He made a retreat of fifteen days in the seminary at Boulogne, and a third general Confession, that he might do the will of God. He took with him the Bishop's recommendation and a letter from a friend of the Prior, and went straight to the monastery.

The Prior consented to let the young postulant make another trial, but he was first to return and take leave of his family.

At Amettes Benedict fell seriously ill. Directly he was able to walk, he bid a last farewell to his parents.

'Whatever,' he said impressively, 'may be the issue of this journey, we shall not again meet in the world.'

Spiritual souls admired Benedict's firmness, they saw in it a clear sign of a true vocation. Others held a different opinion, and criticised his conduct severely; they pitied the parents of such an obstinate son, who, instead of being a help and comfort as he grew up, was only eager to get away from home, to indulge, they thought, a taste for idleness.

This is not the first time that one of God's Saints has been misjudged by those nearest to him.

Benedict left the paternal roof forever on the 12th of August, 1769.

The young Saint went in implicit obedience, his attraction was elsewhere.

Scarcely was he again in his cell, when the former troubles seized him with renewed violence. Despite these attacks he remained calm, affable, full of zeal, exact in every particular of the rule. Not a fault, not an omission could be charged against him; he was a source of edification in every duty.

But the experienced religious quickly saw that his vocation was not to their life. After six weeks it was made known to him by the Prior, Henry Joseph Cappe.

'My son,' he said, 'we see clearly that God has not called you to our institute, you must follow the inspirations of His grace and go where it leads you.'

On the day Benedict came out, the 2nd of October, he wrote the following letter to his parents, charging the servant of the monastery, who accompanied him to Montreuil, to deliver it to them; he started alone, on foot, for la Trappe.

A verse from the 'Miserere' headed the letter. 'From my iniquity and from my sin cleanse me, for my iniquity I know; From my iniquity and from sin.'

> My very dear Father, and my very dear Mother,
> I must tell you that the Carthusians have not found me suitable to their Order. I am, therefore, come out today, October 2nd. I take it as a command from Divine Providence. The Carthusians themselves told me that the hand of God is directing this. I go on my way then towards la Trappe, the goal I have so long wished to reach. I ask your pardon for all the trouble I have caused you, and for my many acts of disobedience. I beg of you both to give me your blessing so that Our Lord may go with me. Every day of my life I shall pray for you. Do not be uneasy on my account. However much I might have wished to remain in

the monastery, they would not have consented to keep me, so I rejoice that the All-Powerful leads me. Be careful for the instruction of my brothers and sisters, especially of my godchild. With the grace of God I shall cost you nothing more, and I will give you no trouble. I commend myself to your prayers. I am well. I have given no money to the servant who takes this letter. Before leaving the monastery I received the sacraments. Let us always serve the good God and He will never forsake us. Take good care of your health. Do read and practise all that Pére l'Aveugle (Pére Lejeune) teaches. His book points the way to heaven, and if we are not guided by it, we cannot hope for salvation. Meditate upon the fearful pains of hell which are the penalty of a single mortal sin that we commit so easily. Strive to be among the small number of the elect. I thank you for all the goodness you have shown me, and for all the services you have rendered me. God will reward you for them. Try to give my brothers and sisters the education you have given me, it is a means to make them happy hereafter. Without instruction one cannot be saved. I have cost you much, but be assured that by God's grace I will profit by all you have done for me. Do not be distressed because I have left the Carthusians, it is not lawful to resist the will of God, and He has thus disposed of me for my greater good, and for my salvation. Remember me to my brothers and sisters. Grant me your blessing. I will not give you any more pain. The good God whom I received before leaving the monastery will assist me, and guide me in the enterprise which is His own inspiration. I will always have the fear of God before my eyes, and His love in my heart. My strong hope is to be taken at la Trappe; in any case I am assured the order at Sept-Fonts is less severe, and that younger postulants are received, but I shall be received at la Trappe.

Your very humble Servant, Benedict Joseph Labre. Montreuil, October 2nd, 1769.

This letter is remarkable for the tenderness and gratitude to his parents; his perfect resignation, and the child-like trust in God which no affliction, cross, or disappointment could diminish. After numberless sufferings and vicissitudes he reached la Trappe; hospitality was given, but beyond that, a firm refusal; he was not twenty-four, and the rule could not be infringed.

EIGHTY MILES FARTHER TO THE ABBEY OF SEPT-FONTS

Thus his second weary journey to Mortagne was fruitless in regard to his hopes, but we may not say so in regard to his merit; he received each rebuff, as it came, straight from God. There was no thought of turning back; from the depths of his self-abasement he made fervent acts of faith and hope, and without a moment's hesitation went forward. The thought of turning back never entered his mind. He arrived at the Abbey of Sept-Fonts on October 30th, 1769, was allowed to speak to the Superior, and with great simplicity told him his experiences. The young stranger's sincerity and piety were so evident, that on the 2nd of November he was allowed to make his formal petition before the Chapter; on the 11th he received the habit as a choir novice, taking the name of Frère Urbain. His humility, regularity and his austerity edified the whole community. At

Sept-Fonts the rule of Saint Benedict was strictly observed; no less austere than that at la Trappe. At this Frère Urbain rejoiced.

For some months joy flooded his soul; the days passed swiftly in prayer and meditation and holy obedience. His spirit of mortification astounded the professed brethren, the grace and readiness with which he adapted himself to all requirements endeared him to the community. The other young novices gladly took him as their model. He gave the greatest edification.

It was the will of God, nevertheless, that he should pass for the third time through the dark night of interior desolation. A wave of tribulation swept over him, not a ray of comfort shone upon his soul. He was troubled by scruples, and accused himself of defects that had absolutely no existence save in his over-wrought imagination. His very humility turned against him, causing him to think himself unworthy to go to Communion, because his contrition for these imagined faults was not, he thought, deep enough.

We are led to wonder why this ardent, devout young soul should have been thus checked in his holy aspirations, and so heavily clouded.

There is only one answer to the question, and that the true solution.

It is that blessed Benedict's course was already traced for him by the finger of God. The halt at Sept-Fonts was but a stage of progression. The desert was to be his portion, a desert in the midst of civilisation, where he was to practise poverty more absolute, solitude more complete, than under the most severe monastic rule. He was in training for his unique vocation.

At the end of six months his health, never robust, gave way under the strain of these sufferings. He was taken into the infirmary in high fever. The religious looked upon him already as a Saint; the doctors assured them that his constitution was not equal to his zeal, and would fail under the rule. It was then decided to remove him to the hospital for the poor outside the monastery, where he could receive better nourishment.

This sentence cut, as it were, the ground from under his feet. The cloistered haven at Seven-Fountains [Sept-Fons] was his last resource, he had hoped to live and die within the shelter of these hallowed walls. Ill as he was, his bodily strength gone, racked by fever, on hearing that he was to be put forth upon the world, he raised his eyes to Heaven, his hands meekly folded on his breast, he simply breathed out the words, 'My God, Thy will be done.'

The hospital attendants said that his life was a continuous conversation with God; they grew tenderly attached to this young patient. They would ask the fathers by turn to visit him, with the invitation, 'Come and see young Labre, he is a Saint.' In his convalescence he waited upon the other patients in total forgetfulness of self. After two months treatment he had to quit his new friends, and to depart from the monastery. There are novices who might have felt this decree to be harsh, even cruel; Benedict's heart knew no such sentiment, it was too full of the love of God, although he could not restrain his tears, when he knelt to receive his Superior's last blessing. In bidding him farewell, Father Abbot used almost the same words as the Prior of Neuville, 'My son, you are not destined for our monastery, God wills you elsewhere.'

The Abbot gave Benedict an open letter to his parents explaining his reason for parting from so exemplary a novice. He also gave him a certificate which Benedict carried about him to his life's end. After his death it was kept at Rome, but has since been given back to the Abbey at Sept-Fonts. The letter to his parents was never delivered. Benedict showed it in 1772 to a Priest at Cossignano, Don Michael Angelo Santucci.

The Abbot naturally supposed that his ex-novice would return to Amettes. Benedict had told the brother infirmarian of an intention to go to Rome; in that direction he turned his steps with profound meekness and resignation, with faith that never faltered, and unflinching courage.

In a second letter written later, the Abbot of Sept-Fonts laid stress upon the excessive delicacy of Benedict's conscience, which kept him in constant fear of offending God.

From Chicri, in Piedmont, the pilgrim wrote a last letter to his parents to allay the anxiety he knew they must feel. This time he signed himself 'your very affectionate son'.

A short time after the letter was sent came a swift illumination, a rift in the spiritual cloud that hung over him. He knew at once that this was the answer to his constant prayers. He did not try to pierce farther into the future, to inquire what lay beyond the gleam. It was enough just to follow, simply to go where the hand of God should lead him. All tormenting scruples vanished. His failure in the novitiate had left a deep wound in his fervent heart, he thought himself rejected because not worthy to lead the religious life of the cloister. That aching pain was healed in an instant and forever.

As in a lightning flash his vocation was revealed. He understood that, like Saint Alexis, he should abandon his country, his kindred, ease and comfort, all that pleases or flatters the senses, to lead a new kind of life; a life most painful, most penitential; not in a wilderness, not in the cloister; but in the midst of the civilised world; devoutly visiting as a pilgrim the renowned sanctuaries.

He took the advice of experienced directors upon this inspiration, and was told he might safely follow it. He obeyed literally the invitation: 'If any one will come after Me, let him deny himself, and take up his cross, and follow Me.'

Here then was the pilgrim, detached from every link of human affection or support; with neither roof to shelter him, nor means to supply his daily needs, frugal as they were. He set forth upon his life's pilgrimage, clothed in an old coat, a rosary in his hands, another upon his neck, the crucifix upon his breast, his arms folded over it.

A small wallet thrown over one shoulder held all his earthly possessions: these were a Testament, his breviary, which he recited every day, the Imitation, and some other books of piety. Of linen and goods he took none. He left all things for prayer and mortification; to live solitary, in the midst of the world.

Steadily he went forward, without haste, or anxiety, heeding neither rain nor snow, cold nor heat. He slept in the open air, sometimes upon straw, oftener upon the bare ground. He avoided the wayside inns, for there his recollection might be disturbed by noise, by travellers' talk, by their songs, perhaps by, what he dreaded more than anything in life, blasphemy.

He never wavered in his belief that this was the path appointed for him to tread; no doubt or perplexity ever again beset his mind on the score of his vocation. As time went on, priests and others, who wished to befriend him, would urge him to change his mode of life, pointing out that he was not making a right use of his youth, and of the talents and gifts which God had given him.

He met all remonstrance on the subject with the meek and quiet answer: It is the Will of God.

On his journey to Rome he halted at all places that held some religious memory dear to the faithful. He lived by charity from day to day, yet never begged, nor reserved anything for the morrow. For nourishment, a piece of bread satisfied him, with herbs, or food that otherwise would have been thrown away: he took barely sufficient to sustain life in the body which he held under such rigid mortification.

If alms were abundant he gave all to the poor. Often he was

the sport of children and of rude persons, who, seeing him, apparently a beggar, bestow charity upon others, concluded that he was out of his senses.

Mockery never troubled his sweet serenity, he bore all with patience and even love. He rejoiced in suffering humiliations. His renunciation of self went beyond mere externals: he had gifts of intelligence and knowledge, but chose to pass as a poor mendicant, totally ignorant: he wished to be unknown, and despised as an abject for Christ's sake. The Divine model was ever before his eyes, never absent from his thoughts; his heart, mind, soul and strength, were concentrated upon the Redeemer with adoring love and gratitude.

Most of us find a certain sense of gratification in being well dressed; others are content to feel that at least their costume is neither unsuitable nor ridiculous; a few are too indolent to care.

Saint Benedict Labre did not belong to any of these classes. His keen French instinct of good taste, elegance, and propriety caused him to be fully alive to the advantages of dress. He had always shown a love of order and regularity in his home life. He now wore the garb of extreme poverty, and neglected his appearance, not because he was slovenly or indolent. It was his deliberate choice to cover himself with rags and ridicule, so as to crush and destroy every germ of self-esteem.

When he left Sept-Fonts, fever was still upon him, his health was not sufficiently restored to cope with his chosen regime. Before reaching Loretto he had to spend three weeks in a hospital.

HIS FIRST VISIT TO LORETTO

The holy house of Nazareth—transported by angels to Loretto—drew his steps to that frequented shrine. He was seen passing slowly through the town; there was dignity in his bearing, despite his exhaustion; his tattered garment was a strange contrast to his young face, emaciated, but delicate and refined.

Prostrate in that miraculously preserved sanctuary which had sheltered Jesus, Mary and Joseph, the pilgrim Saint spent hours rapt in meditation and prayer, motionless, absorbed.

At Loretto, as in the Basilicas of Rome, there are confessors who speak all the European languages, ready to hear the numerous pilgrims who arrive from all parts. Benedict went to the French confessor, Father Andrew Bodetti, who, after hearing this singularly devout penitent, was anxious to relieve his too evident destitution.

The church was served by Jesuit Fathers, and a distribution of food was made every day to the needy who received tickets. A fund left by Cardinal Joyeuse for the relief of poor French pilgrims was also administered. Father Bodetti arranged in his own mind that his penitent should benefit by both these charities. He pointed Benedict out to Brother Laurence Cayla, telling him to have care of that young man, for he was a devout soul. Brother Laurence hastened to overtake him, and first offered him a bed at the hospice. The pilgrim gently but firmly declined. The brother insisted upon his taking food, shoes, clothes and money.

These were refused. 'I thank you, I thank you,' said the low musical voice: 'there are others more needy than I. Will you kindly keep it for them.'

This brother was charged to distribute the charities; he tried again and again to induce Benedict to accept help; his efforts were fruitless.

Benedict had made a resolution not to accept material aid from his confessors, and from this rule he would not swerve. He spent eight or ten days at Loretto, passing his whole days in the Santa Casa (Holy House) and when the doors were shut, he slept upon the ground near the church.

On the 18th of November he was at Assisi kneeling at the tomb of Saint Francis, drawn there doubtless by the wish to place his life under the patronage of the Seraphic Father, that ardent apostle of holy poverty. There also he approached the Sacraments, and had his name placed upon the register of the Arch-Confraternity, and was girded with the cord which he wore till his death. He received it from the hands of Père Joseph Marie Temple, who later was to know much more of this young pilgrim.

From Assisi he crossed the mountains on foot in the rainy season.

On the 3rd of December, 1770, he entered the gates of Rome. 'Beautiful Rome, holy city!' was his salutation, which he was often afterwards heard to repeat as he became acquainted with all its sources of devotion and noble sanctuaries.

He passed the first three days in the hospital of Saint Louis, founded in 1478 for poor French pilgrims; afterwards he spent his days in the Churches meditating upon the Passion of our Lord. Here his aspirations were fulfilled, his spirit lifted to the very portal of Heaven. The unceasing practice of prayer with mortification caused him to advance with rapid strides upon the path of sanctity. His whole life was a prayer. He treated his body simply as a contemptible vehicle to convey him from one shrine to another, where his soul gathered to itself the essence of devotion, as a bee draws out sweetness from the flowers.

His shelter at night was sometimes a hole in a wall upon the Quirinal, or an arch in the Coliseum. He loved that soil hallowed by the blood of martyrs. Early morn found him waiting at the doors of one or other of the Basilicas, till they were opened; he heard Masses until twelve o'clock. Then he would go with others of the poor to some Convent where soup was distributed. He did this to conform to their customs. He preferred to pick up in the streets enough remnants of food to allay hunger.

In the afternoon he would be at the Scala Santa (Holy Stairs), or in the Church wherever the Forty Hours' Exposition was taking place; he would often obtain leave to pass the night in adoration before the Blessed Sacrament.

As he left the different Churches, he would recite the Miserere. At the corners of the streets he saluted the pictures and statues of the Virgin with touching reverence, often stopping before them, and turning back to gaze upon them as he breathed out an invocation, 'Ma mere! O Marie! Ma mere!'

Towards the end of May, 1771, he made his second pilgrimage to Loretto, passing by way of Fabriano, where the body of Saint Romuald, founder of the Camaldolese is venerated.

On the feast of Saint Anthony of Padua, which is celebrated with great devotion at Fabriano, the Rector of Saint James' Chapel,

Fr Marius Pogetti, on entering, early in the morning, saw a poor man upon his knees absorbed in prayer. His face and attitude were like a fervent religious, but the man's clothing bore no resemblance to a habit. He wore a grey garment girded on the loins by a cord, from which hung a small wooden bowl. A short cape or cloak covered his shoulders. A crucifix of copper hung against his breast, a large rosary was upon his neck; his wallet, very flat and empty, was on the ground beside him. The priest was attracted and touched by the man's perseverance in prayer. During all the masses and ceremonies he knelt immoveable, his eyes fixed upon the altar or the Tabernacle. At noon, when the church was deserted, the sacristan, Vincent Brunetti, saw him still kneeling, his arms outstretched in the form of a cross. To the Rector's amazement when the doors were about to be closed for the night, the man politely and gently asked leave to remain where he was during the night.

'You shall lodge,' said the Rector, 'in the hospital for priests and travellers attached to this chapel; there you will be under the same roof as the Tabernacle.'

Knowing that the man had eaten nothing all day Fr Marius Pogetti told the sacristan to take him some food, and a light.

Benedict availed himself of the shelter, but did not use the bed. At dawn he was again in the church praying before a beautiful statue of Saint James. He went to confession, after which the Rector did not hesitate to allow him to serve his mass, miserably clad as he was. To serve mass had ever been the joy of Benedict's life. Those who were present told Fr Pogetti that a Saint had served his mass that morning.

The charitable priest was eager to supply him with food, clothes, and money, and was displeased by his firm refusals. 'The poor,' said Benedict, 'should live on what they may gather from day to day; besides I need so little to nourish this poor body.'

The humble young stranger had already been remarked in the churches and in the streets for his wonderful piety and recollection. Instead of jeers, generous alms were offered to him, and were refused. It was in Fr Pogetti's chapel, dedicated to the apostle, that Benedict resolved to visit the shrine of Saint James at Compostello. He did nothing without the sanction of a director, so some days before he left the small town of Fabriano he came to the sacristy door of Saint James', and in his modest, reverent way said to Fr Marius Pogetti that he wished to make a general confession. A day was fixed, and at the appointed time the penitent arrived. The Rector—who afterwards was a witness during the process of information—thus gives his testimony:

> 'I had the happiness of hearing this confession, and of learning the whole history of his life from the time he was under the tuition of one of his uncles in France. By my interrogation and his answers, I understood that, despite temptations, and the assaults of the demon, he had kept his baptismal innocence intact. I was singularly moved and edified, and I had no difficulty in uniting my opinion to that which had been formed of this holy soul.'

Benedict's object was to be directed in his project of going to Compostello. The director approved of it; he recognised the inspiration of God in this extraordinary life. It appeared to him marked by the impress of the divine will, so that he did not for a moment think of advising this young man to change the humiliating, painful existence he had adopted. On the contrary, in listening to him Fr Pogetti said he felt himself lifted above all material considerations, and he could only exhort this admirable penitent to persevere in his abjection, and to go his way, as a pilgrim and mendicant, on which he had entered so generously.

Benedict accepted shelter at the hospital or guest house for fifteen nights during his stay at Fabriano, but without using the bed, or taking food of any kind, except a little of what the sacristan brought him on the first occasion.

BENEDICT'S DISCOURSE

On the 23rd of June Benedict was in one of the streets of Fabriano under a torrent of rain. A pious widow, Vincenta Rocca, invited him to take shelter in her house. He came in with the salutation he always used: Praised be Jesus and Mary. The children grouped themselves round him and he made them a beautiful little address.

Someone present asked, 'How ought we to love God?'

'To love Him properly,' said Benedict, 'we want three hearts in one. The first should be aflame with love towards God, to make us think of Him continually, to speak to Him, to act as He wills, and above all to bear with patience the ills it may please Him to send us during our life.

'The second should be all flesh towards our neighbour; it should urge us to help him in his spiritual needs by instruction, counsel, example and prayer. It ought to be especially tender towards sinners, and particularly to our enemies, asking the Saviour to enlighten, to lead them to repentance. It should be full of compassion for the souls in Purgatory, entreating Jesus and Mary to bring them into the place of peace.

'The third should be all bronze for ourselves, and abhor every kind of sensuality; it should resist without mercy the love of self, abjure one's own will, and master all the inclinations of our corrupt nature. The more you hate and chastise your flesh, the greater will be your reward in the life to come.'

These are lessons which the Saint carried out to the letter in his own person.

A neighbour named Virginia Fiordi, bed-ridden for nine years in acute suffering, sent to beg the poor man to come and say some consoling words to her.

He moved gently to her bed-side, and stood there a pathetic figure, his arms clasped over the crucifix.

'My daughter,' he said, 'Jesus loves you much; your state far from exciting murmurs and regrets should seem to you enviable. So many Saints have desired to suffer as you suffer, and have not obtained it; good and ills come to us straight from God; try to profit by one as much as the other: prepare to endure, with courage, the burden of a long life of suffering, because it is a sign that in His mercy our Lord prepares an immense weight of eternal glory for you. In putting you to so heavy a trial, He wishes from you a great virtue, and He designs for you an immense reward. For, I repeat, you will pass from this bed into Paradise.'

After Benedict had left the house, his words had made such a happy impression upon her, that she exclaimed, 'I cannot take from my mind the thought that our Lord himself has visited me in the guise of that poor man!'

Hearing that the Poverello (poor man) was in the invalid's house, several neighbours joined the group. Mothers brought their little children; Virginia Fiordi, her sister Romualde; and the widow Vicenta said there was such power and sweetness in his discourse, never had they heard the things of God spoken of like that. His words awoke some dormant secrets of conscience in the bosom of the sufferer. Without supernatural light, she declared, he could not have seen as he did into her heart, nor reveal it to her for the good of her soul. 'Every word he uttered was a consolation of paradise.'

He tenderly warned the little children against disobedience and lies.

'Always tell the truth, if you wish to be like Jesus Christ, who is truth itself.'

He foretold that one child of ten years old would become a Capuchin, and would suffer many crosses, which was afterwards strictly realised.

Before leaving the house he asked for a sheet of paper, and wrote a prayer in Latin which, being Italians, they could quite understand. He gave it to them saying if they recited it with faith their house, and the neighbouring houses would be preserved from lightning, fire, or earthquake.

Ten years later, in 1781, an earthquake destroyed many houses in Fabriano. That of Fiordi and his neighbours were spared. The prayer was:

> Jesus Christ, the King of Glory, came in peace. God was made man. The Word was made flesh. Christ was born of the Virgin Mary. Christ went out from the midst of them in peace. Christ was crucified. Christ died. Christ was buried. Christ rose again. Christ ascended into Heaven. Christ has conquered. Christ reigns. Christ rules. Christ defend us from all evil. Jesus is with us. *Pater. Ave. Gloria.*

It is an epitome of Christ's atonement, and of the Faith.

Leaving this house he went to the Cathedral church of Fabriano, where Vincenta Rocca saw him praying that same evening.

The report of his visit to the poor bed-ridden patient, and what he had said, spread quickly, and Benedict found himself an object of respectful attention, which terrified him. Next day, as he came out of a church in the afternoon, a crowd gathered round him; voices called out that the Poverello was a saint. His one thought was to get away directly; he spent the last night, the 25th June, at the hospital; charged the sacristan to give his grateful thanks to the kind rector, adding some words that were prophetic: 'The good God will pay my debt to the hospital.'

The morrow came, but Benedict did not return. Some time after his departure, a lady at Loretto bequeathed a sum of money to Saint James' Church at Fabriano for the hospice. She was quite unknown at Fabriano; her family was German, and not aware of the existence of the church. The arrival of this legacy caused the poor pilgrim's words to be remembered. His historians say that he passed sometimes through Fabriano on subsequent journeys to Loretto, was even seen praying before the beautiful statue of Saint James; but never again did he speak to anyone in the town where people, he said, had begun to take notice of him, as of something good.

FROM LORETTO, ALONG THE ADRIATIC COAST, AND NAPLES

Benedict paid his visit of devotion to Loretto: thence he passed along the Adriatic, stopping at the various sanctuaries. In towns he slept in hospitals for the poor; in the country, just where he was, under a hedge or bush. In the Basilica of Saint Nicholas of Bari, he prayed the whole morning prostrate before the Saint's tomb. On the signal being given to leave the church, the doors being closed for the midday hour, he rose and went out, his arms crossed over his breast, his invariable attitude. In his course he passed before the prison. A number of glowering faces were pressed against the iron bars of the dungeons to catch a breath of open air. Benedict could hear the sighs and complaints of the unfortunate prisoners. He fell upon his knees in silent prayer for a few moments: then a voice of celestial beauty floated upward, intoning the Litany of the Blessed Virgin—it was his, and it moved some of his unhappy auditors to tears. A crowd of listeners soon collected from all directions; liberal alms were offered. Benedict took them, raised them to his lips by way of thanks, and forthwith distributed them among the prisoners.

Thus was fulfilled his ardent wish to procure them some relief. He used the same means on other occasions when he saw suffering and had nothing to give to relieve it.

On his journeys he often met with derision, sometimes blows. One day a stone struck him which drew blood. He stopped, pressed his arms closer over the crucifix, and without looking whence came the blow he picked up the stone and touched it with his lips as he thought of the ignominies heaped upon his Divine Model. Once after confession, at Quargnento, he said to the priest 'The good God has been too good to me. I have not yet had to bear any ill-treatment for His sake.'

A state of suffering was, in Benedict's opinion, the school for saints.

He would comfort the afflicted by saying 'One must learn to suffer here; think of the reward in heaven!'

Once an old man, having invited him to sit down at his table, wished for a parting word before Benedict left. The clock struck. 'Well,' said the Saint, 'each time you hear that clock strike remember you are not master of the next hour; and think at the same time of the Passion that our Lord Jesus Christ chose to suffer to put us in possession of a joyful eternity.'

On February 13th, 1772, he was at Naples praying at the different shrines, especially at the tomb of Saint Januarius. On the 17th of March he started for Rome, stopping at Monte Cassino to revere the memory of Saint Benedict, his patron. His second sojourn in Rome was short; his life the same as before. Fr Gabrini, of the Church of SS Vincent and Anastasia, near the fountain of Trevi, was his confessor, and soon saw that he had to deal with a privileged soul. Benedict said his profession was that of Pilgrim, that he was a great sinner, and needed help to make a good confession.

For the third time he went to Loretto, passing by way of Port-de-Fermo, and by Cossignano, where the Abbé Michael Angelo Santucci, in his deposition, tells of their meeting. On his way back from saying Mass, the Abbé was struck by the appearance of a stranger leaning against the wall of his house, exhausted, but saying the De Profundis in a low voice. The priest's keen ear caught the French accent, which was marked. The devout tone, the man's youth, his modest, serious, composed countenance, something sweet and noble in his aspect, excited the priest's respect and 'veneration'. He spoke at once, asking the poor man his name and nationality. Benedict replied in French. Abbé Santucci was studying the language, and welcomed this opportunity of exercising it in an act of charity. He invited the wayfarer into his house, but could not induce him to come in without using his authority as a priest. Benedict refused the offered seat earnestly, saying that his garments were too unsuitable, besides some insect might be left.

The priest showed no disgust; he insisted, and half in French, half in Italian he expressed his surprise to see a young man in such a plight who was evidently born and educated to a different state. He asked his history, and Benedict told it with frankness and in as few words as possible.

Every word he spoke deepened the Abbé's interest. 'Why,' he asked, 'did you not go back to your family after leaving Sept-Fonts? One can serve God everywhere.'

'I consulted a confessor,' was the reply, 'and he approved of my design to lead a solitary life as a pilgrim.'

Abbé Santucci pressed Benedict to stay in his house; his pretext was to take lessons in French; he was much more keen to hear this young guest speak on spiritual things. But the pilgrim refused; he did not wish to interrupt his pilgrimages; he was anxious to reach Loretto. In the end he consented to stay a few days at Cossignano, and come morning and evening to speak French with the Abbé. He would sleep at the hospital for poor pilgrims and take his meal with his pupil.

The next morning Benedict said he must start directly for Loretto.

Abbé Santucci drew from him at last that he had suffered anguish from hearing the curses of two pilgrims in the hospital with him.

'I will use my influence with the vicar in charge, and have you lodged in that part of the hospice kept for priests. You will have a room to yourself, so do not go yet.' Benedict's reverence for the priesthood made him comply with the young Abbé's request, so the lessons continued.

Pupil and teacher read sermons together, which they discussed. Abbé Michael was amazed at his poor teacher's enlightened and spiritual comments. He seemed to enjoy these conversations, speaking freely upon all religious subjects; but if any other topic was broached, any allusion made to his family or country, Benedict became brief and silent. He willingly spoke of his time as a novice at Sept-Fonts.

Every moment apart from these lessons was spent in the church. The poverello served the Abbé's mass. Once after consecration his glance fell upon the poor man kneeling there, his hands joined, his head inclined, his attitude and bearing expressive of rapt devotion. Abbé Santucci's edification was so great, he said later, that he blushed, and was ashamed to think that a poor layman served Mass with greater fervour than he, a priest, could celebrate it.

Benedict would never walk beside the Abbé though

constantly invited to do so; sometimes he was impatiently beckoned forward, but respect kept him always at a certain distance behind. On one occasion, during their spiritual reading, Benedict's deep blue eyes filled with tears. 'Oh,' he exclaimed, '*if people offend God, it is because they do not know His goodness; he who knows it will never sin.*'

Abbé Santucci's family and friends were not pleased he should show this regard for an unknown and miserable tramp; they besought him to be more prudent in his charity. Their counsels were unheeded; the priest only longed to make Benedict known to all who were able to appreciate the wonders of God. But as the saint dreaded nothing so much as any mark of esteem, his humility made him refuse to visit even one of the Abbé's friends who was ill.

He asked his benefactor to dismiss him—as if he were a servant.

Abbé Santucci, daily more impressed by the wisdom and goodness of this rare character, felt real affection for him, and very reluctantly saw him depart after ten days' acquaintance. At first he had suggested to Benedict that he ought to take some care of himself with regard to cleanliness and dress, nor did he understand Benedict's objections; he reproached him for neglect.

In obedience Benedict accepted the clothes that were given, and wore the shirt; but no persuasion could make him put off his ragged coat; he gave to other poor the clothes he did not use.

On the morning he left Cossignano he served Abbé Santucci's Mass, and after the thanksgiving went his way. The priest accompanied him some distance out of the town, and put silver into his hand for the journey, which Benedict instantly gave back; he would only take a few pence. Thanking his benefactor, he took his hand to kiss it—after the Italian custom—with so much grace, humility, and reverence, that tears rushed to the priest's eyes; he turned quickly, and on reaching home shut himself in his room to give free vent to the grief he felt at the loss of this friend. He had asked Benedict to write to him—no letter ever came. The saint ruthlessly cut every tie of earthly affection or friendship. Only after death was his motive for this apparent forgetfulness explained. Abbé Santucci was several years in Rome, not aware of Benedict's presence there; but afterwards, when the city rang with the fame of the dead saint, Benedict Joseph Labre, then he recognised his pilgrim friend whom he had loved and admired so much, and worked zealously for his honour and beatification.

BENEDICT IS THREATENED WITH IMPRISONMENT AS A VAGRANT

Benedict reached Loretto June 3rd, 1772. His time was spent before the Blessed Sacrament, invoking Mary's prayers.

Wherever he went, even passing through a village, his first care was to go straight to the church. He prayed for the conversion of sinners and unbelievers, and for the deliverance of the souls in purgatory. Hundreds of intentions were recommended to the benefit of his prayers: he was most scrupulous in the fulfilment of these obligations. From Loretto he again went to Assisi, and retired for a time to Mont Alverno, where he made a general confession to prepare himself for the long, painful pilgrimage to Spain. He crossed France, was at Moulins in the beginning of 1773, stayed there till after Easter, visited Sept-Fonts several times, but without making himself known. God showed his sanctity by various signs. At Moulins, when distributing bread and peas to the poor, the food multiplied in his hands.

A pious Christian, M. Fanjon, who gave him shelter, was the victim of a dangerous malady; a sudden access came on. Benedict hearing him say, 'I suffer intensely; this, no doubt, will be my end,' began to pray in a low voice.

'Master,' he said, presently, 'it will be nothing; it will pass.' And so it did, entirely; during the ten years that he lived after, Fanjon suffered no more from it.

Benedict would read aloud some pious book, or follow out his own meditations, to shorten the long winter evenings, while under Fanjon's roof. The family gladly listened as his clear, soft voice dilated upon the goodness and attributes of God. It prevented useless and frivolous conversation. Devout curiosity could not refrain from watching this singular visitor. He was seen to descend from the loft at daybreak to go to the church, where nearly his whole day was spent. He ate only once, after sundown, taking bread moistened with water. When he had retired to his granary for the night, he was heard to flagellate himself severely. The scourge that he used, small cords with little points of metal, was seen hidden in the straw upon which he slept.

A prophet is without honour in his own country! Benedict suffered at Moulins a kind of persecution. His charitable host was blamed for receiving him. The vicar of the church he frequented was annoyed at the constant presence of this poor, unclean personage, whose piety he thought exaggerated, if not hypocritical.

Benedict was even threatened with imprisonment. He met all this with silence and resignation; but fearing to bring trouble upon those who sheltered him, he took leave of them, and went out under the wintry sky, his way-worn feet continuing the journey to Spain. Having no care for his body, he was undaunted by perils of the way, or by inclemency of weather.

When urged to take some provision for his need, and not give away everything to the other poor, he said, 'God, who has fed me today, will know how to provide for me tomorrow.'

PRISON, AND THE CROWN OF THORNS

In the Pyrenees, passing through a wood near Saint Bertrand-de-Comminges, he came upon a traveller lying by the roadside. He had been robbed and wounded by brigands. The pilgrim knelt down beside him, and was tenderly dressing the wounds. While engaged in this act of charity, soldiers came up. Benedict, suspected of being the assassin, was seized and thrown into prison. He was afterwards released, for the wounded man recovered to recognise his benefactor.

Benedict's passage is traced and remembered in Barcelona, at Notre Dame de Montserrat, Manresa, Notre Dame du Pilier, in Saragossa, at Burgos, where there is a miraculous crucifix, and at Saint James of Compostela, the chief object of this pilgrimage. He there made three novenas in honour of the Blessed Trinity, towards Whom he became more devout every day. So true is it that the *practice* of piety improves in us what is good, and preserves what is improved!

He returned by Bilbao, is remembered at Montpelier, Lunel, Arles, Aix, Marseilles, Nice, Frejus. Wherever the poor pilgrim passed, he edified all by his devotion, his humility, his mortification.

At Frejus, one evening a poor man in tatters was seen leaving the cathedral, moving with great difficulty, his legs swathed in old bandages that covered neglected sores. Under the fine trees near was a barber's shop. It is not known whether the sufferer ventured in, or was invited, but at any rate he was welcomed. The master, who was also a surgeon, offered with great charity to attend to the offensive wounds. He cleansed and dressed them most carefully. Christian pity urged him to extend his ministration to the head and hair, regardless of insects, only too apparent. The pilgrim's gratitude was equal to the immense charity shown towards him. He promised to pray for the family, and assured them that the blessing of God would follow all they undertook. The good surgeon was not alone in his respect and admiration; to this day, Saint Benedict Joseph Labre's memory is preserved. Facts testified to his power. The surgeon's family was extraordinarily blessed. It became one of the most opulent and honourable in the town, and held many important positions.

Blessings of all kinds were sent from Heaven upon those who gave shelter, or in any way ministered to Benedict, the poor servant of God.

He was well known at Paray-le-Monial, was revered for his sanctity not only by the Community of the Visitation and hospital, but by the townspeople. It is stated that the Abbé de Garennes, chaplain of the hospital, was the confessor who first approved of Benedict's mode of life. He was a priest of good family, vowed, by his own choice, to poverty, and the service of the poor.

The Sisters of the Visitation said that 'it was from the tomb of Saint Margaret Mary Alacoque that this holy pilgrim went forth to win Heaven, by the most complete disdain of earthly things that can be imagined.'

So great was their veneration for him that a Sister of the Hospital, Marie Louise de Labaille, gathered up some crumbs she found in his wallet, and agreed with the other sisters to put them in their soup, for the nourishment of their souls more than their bodies.

At Lunel he called at the hospital of the Sisters of Charity. His first act was to prostrate before the statue of the Blessed Virgin. He was invited to take food, but instead of eating, his eyes were fixed upon the crucifix attached to the Sister's rosary hanging at her side. She asked what drew his attention. He said, 'It is the crown of thorns in the centre of the cross.'

'If you like, I will give it to you.'

'Oh! I should be so happy to have it.'

She detached it from the rosary, and gave it to him; he placed it on his breast. Her kindness was rewarded by many blessings that followed Benedict's visit to the house. The Sister attributed her recovery from a serious illness to his prayers. When he was dying, she knew the exact moment; it was revealed to her, and she announced it to the community in the words, 'Jesus Christ's poor one has gone to receive his reward.'

A Lazariste Father told her that he had seen her crucifix with the crown of thorns in the hands of a mendicant, who said it was given to him by a Sister of Charity, whom he never forgot in his prayers.

In the course of his journeys he passed the city of Lyons, no doubt to visit Notre Dame de Fourvieres. A family in a village near gave him shelter and a kind welcome into their house. The place where he used to sit is shown, between the window and spacious hearth, in the large front room where the inmates gathered for the evening meal. At the extreme end of this room is an alcove. Several years after the Saint's death, in that alcove was born Jean Baptiste Vianney, Curé d'Ars, another great servant of God, whose life seems to show what blessed Benedict's would have been had he entered the Priesthood. The parents of Jean Baptiste saw in this pious pilgrim a representative of our Lord.

Benedict slept in their stable; and later, their own son, Jean Baptiste, used to sleep there when his occupation was to tend sheep.

Who can wonder if graces descended upon him in answer to the prayers which had been poured forth in that stable for God's glory! To reward also the parents, who had shown spontaneous charity to 'one of these His least brethren.'

Wherever blessed Benedict went the priests who received his countless confessions held but one opinion, that this was a great soul of the good God. Some were so moved and edified by what they saw and heard of him, that they wrote down the impressions left upon their minds by his passage through their town or village.

At Quargnento, a Canon of the Church, to whom he confessed, and who afterwards invited him into his house, that he might learn more of this beautiful soul, said of him: 'He goes to Rome to become holy, but he is a saint already. His face when I spoke with him seemed to me like that of Jesus, it was so celestial and gracious.'

The Canon accompanied him some distance out of the village, and on taking leave Benedict gave him a little book. This meeting made a deep impression on the priest; he took notes of their conversation, and when dying he gave them into his sister's charge, as they might be useful for God's glory.

Upon the booklet he wrote, 'Given by a devout French pilgrim who had left all things, and his country, to live as a hermit under the direction of a confessor.'

The booklet, which had belonged to Benedict, the Canon once placed on his heart when suffering from an aneurism, and it cured him instantly. His sister was cured of a convulsion by the same means.

Many miracles of this kind are recorded.

Passing through the town of Gray, Benedict saw a youth fall into the Saone. Benedict could not swim, but immediately plunged into the river and rescued him. Some time afterwards the parents begged Benedict to obtain the cure of their son. A severe illness had followed the accident, from the effects of which he still suffered. Complete recovery was the result.

In many ways God's good providence came to His servant's help. On one occasion when he was returning to Rome in 1772, after having crossed the Apennines during winter, he visited Naples, Saint Januarius, and Monte Cassino; passing through a village he was faint from fatigue.

An inn-keeper offered him a little wine, which the Saint accepted as a gift of charity. But the man expected to be paid, and when he found the poor traveller had no money began to blaspheme. Benedict shrank from no outrage or abuse to himself, but to hear the name of God blasphemed made him tremble with unspeakable anguish. He raised his eyes to Heaven. The glass was no longer empty, it was filled with wine. God is never outdone in generosity. It is not surprising that He should respond by a miracle to the appeal of one who had left all things for His company; who sought Him with ardour that never flagged; with constancy that no obstacle could daunt. One who had thrown off every trammel of the body, even the lawful and necessary care that a human frame demands, so that his spirit might be free to soar after the things which are unseen, spiritual and eternal.

Life in Rome

Benedict re-entered Rome on Easter day, April 3rd, 1774. Fatigue had reduced him to a pitiful state; only by leaning heavily on his staff could he drag himself along. After three days of devotion he appeared at the hospital Saint Louis, his legs being covered with sores.

A compatriot was in the hospital who knew Benedict's parents, and offered to take them a letter, if he would write it, to console them. 'Tell them that I am happy; give them my remembrance; it is not necessary to write,' he replied, thus resisting a temptation to connect the link to home-life, so heroically broken.

Three days were the limit allowed to pilgrims to stay at the hospital. He was quite ready to go forth again to resume his habitual stern rule of life, passing the chilly nights in a hole in the wall of a house on the Quirinal, under an outside staircase, which formed a little arch.

A priest, Don Carlo Carezani, saw him emerge early one morning from this shelter, and thought how degraded must be the being reduced to this. When the man stood upright Don Carezani saw, to his sorrow and disgust, that though clothed in rags, he was extremely young. But his face was a most striking contrast to his condition: it was calm and dignified; there was upon it no expression of suffering or misery. His bearing was polite and reserved. Without taking notice of anything round him, he signed himself with the cross, and continued his prayers. 'Ah,' thought the priest, 'God be praised, this is one of His servants.'

Later, Don Carezani was to know more of the Saint, for he became one of his confessors.

Benedict had chosen this refuge to be near a beautiful mosaic of the Blessed Virgin, visible from the square of Monte Cavallo—as Romans call the Quirinal. The Swiss Guards on duty before the palace, seeing him gaze upon this picture with intense devotion for half-an-hour together, sometimes treated him as a fool, and would roughly order him away. Ragged and sordid garments were a most unusual sight in Rome, where the very poor were clothed by the charity of their richer neighbours. Self-respect and industry made others careful to preserve a decent appearance. Observant Romans, struck by the beauty of holiness upon his young, emaciated features, began to notice his presence in the city. Devout persons were filled with veneration when they saw him in the churches leaving the confessional, but above all when he received Holy Communion. Other poor did not look upon him as one like themselves: they thought he was some person of high birth, under a vow to lead a penitential life. A good woman, named Maria Dominica Bravi, who had remarked him on his first visit to Rome, held this opinion. She was deeply impressed by his sanctity, and touched also by his great destitution. 'I saw him,' she says, 'so extenuated that I thought "he does all this penance and lacks what is necessary to preserve life."'

A young priest, Abbé Stuter, who belonged to the association called the 'Evangelical Work', approached Benedict, inviting him to attend the meetings. This work was for the instruction of the very poor. They were assembled on certain days to make the Stations of the Cross, recite the rosary, be instructed in their faith, and receive a small alms. Often they were taken to the Coliseum, or the Holy Stairs, or one of the churches.

When this was explained to Benedict he was greatly edified, as indeed he was by all he saw in Rome. The number of churches, the sacred statues, the devotion of the people, and the care taken for the instruction of the poor.

'*Belle Rome, Sainte ville!* Beautiful Rome, Holy City!' he repeated with joy.

During the religious exercises the priest remarked his deep piety, his attention, and the modesty of his habitual attitude, his eyes cast down, his hands crossed over his breast. But he also remarked that Benedict stood apart from the others. The rule was that they should be in a group. Abbé Stuter thought this was a touch of pride; he ordered the saint to join the others. Benedict obeyed; the priest could see, however, that it was distasteful to him, and asked his reason.

'I come,' he replied, 'to hear the Word of God. I do not wish for the alms.' His rule was never to let any material advantage be joined to his devotions. His threadbare garment was a proof that he should not despise the smallest offering, therefore the Abbé still suspected pride when he found nothing would induce his poor man to take the money. Benedict was always the first to arrive at these meetings, and if at the Coliseum, he would retire into the hermit guardians little chapel to pray.

His first visit to the Holy Stairs was made with these companions; he practised silence so absolutely that only by degrees he discovered the abundant sanctuaries and shrines of Rome. Works of piety carried on in the squares attracted him first. It was there he joined the 'Urban Mission,' founded by a Jesuit Father in 1606, to reach those who did not frequent the churches. They were collected in the squares by some eloquent preacher, and led in procession to one of the twelve churches chosen for the month's pious exercises. The Urban Mission continued the whole year. When questioned upon his faith and doctrine, Benedict's answers showed such a profound knowledge of both that his instructors quickly understood that he was no ordinary poor man.

The other poor at that time called him *le monsieur*, the French gentleman: his accent betrayed his nationality. Many persons believed him to be a Jesuit, who had suffered when the Order was suppressed in France.

The Abbé Stuter says, 'When Benedict recited the acts of faith, hope, and charity, his tones showed that they came from the depth of his soul, that his heart felt what his lips uttered. During the exhortations he stood with his eyes cast down, his hands crossed over his breast, more like a seraph than a creature of earth.' The Abbé lived close to Monte Cavallo, and had many opportunities of learning to know the Saint better. He began to understand the extent of his mortification when he saw him at midday making his repast on bits of bread picked from the pavement or refuse heap. He noticed him often at the door of the Visitation Convent, apart from the other poor, waiting till the distribution of food had been made, and the provisions gone! He gave a proof of his docility when Abbé Stuter spoke to him about the damp, unhealthy place he had chosen to sleep in. The saint left it at once, and passed his nights on the steps of the Basilica Saint Mary Major. Afterwards he found shelter in the Coliseum, under the arch nearest to the little chapel, where he gathered a little straw, and spent more than half the night in prayer. Visitors coming to see the Coliseum by moonlight were sometimes startled to see a kneeling figure absorbed in meditation.

If they asked in astonishment or pity: 'What are you doing here?'

Without moving or looking up, he would reply, 'I am doing the will of God.'

The devout Dominica Bravi ventured to speak to him one day. She had brought some bread, and two eggs kept warm in a cloth, which she offered. He declined the food with a movement of his head. 'It is Thursday,' she urged, 'the day on which Jesus Christ ate with His Apostles. I cannot of myself order you to take it, but do as if God commanded you, in obedience.'

Dominica had hit the right chord. God and obedience were two words he could never hear unmoved. He lifted his eyes to heaven.

'*Le bon Dieu*, the good God,' he said twice, as he took one of the eggs. 'This is enough.'

Dominica insisted with some more well-chosen words, for she felt her wish to give him food was a holy inspiration.

Benedict could not refuse the charity brought so unexpectedly in the name of God.

Dominica says: 'He reluctantly took the other egg.' She held out the roll she had made herself.

'Ah! the beautiful bread, *bon Dieu*,' he said, in thanksgiving, as he put it into his wallet.

Dominica Bravi had a nephew who was studying in Rome. She was in considerable anxiety with regard to his perseverance and his vocation, and took the opportunity of telling the Saint her fears, and recommended her nephew to his prayers.

Benedict listened; he then advised her to say a *Credo* every time the young man went out of the house.

She faithfully obeyed; and later, when she had the happiness of seeing her nephew a priest, she attributed his preservation and success to the help of her 'holy poor one,' and his wise counsel.

HE RECEIVES ADMIRATION AND INDIGNITY WITH EQUAL UNCONCERN

About this time Benedict frequented the Church of Santa Maria dei Monti; the worshippers were, many of them, poor. One devout person offered to give him clothes. 'Thank you, I do not need them; give them to others. God will reward your charity,' he said with his usual courtesy and decision, but without turning his head. He heard masses all the morning upon his knees, on the epistle side, close to the rail of the high altar.

I, who write, have knelt there; and yet longer on the spot, at the foot of the miraculous statue of the Madonna, where hour after hour found him on his knees, or prostrate in ardent prayer. His mortal remains now lie beneath the stone. One feels it is good to be there. Up till then my veneration for this great Saint was half-reluctant. But something of his spirit seems to hover, to linger, within those walls; to soften, to draw, to stimulate devotion. The most coveted earthly prizes pale and fade into dead ashes at the closer contact of that lofty soul; who went through the world untainted by one temporal desire; who forbore to use, touch, or even look at earth's manifold gifts.

Saint Benedict Joseph Labre acted literally up to the aspiration which many lips repeat in a pious, figurative sense. My God and my All, may the sweet flame of Thy love consume my soul, so that I may die to the world for the love of Thee, Who vouchsafed to die upon the Cross for the love of me. Love for his Divine Master literally consumed blessed Benedict. It possessed him completely. He had won it by crucifying the flesh with holy violence, and he found out that in the conversation of Jesus, 'there was no bitterness, nor in His company any tediousness, but joy and gladness.'

The effect of Benedict's visible presence was to kindle in other hearts the fire of Divine love, after the first impulse of nature's disgust at his poverty and squalor.

It was the habit of an educated man, Antonio Silvani, to go twice a week to the Church of Santa Maria dei Monti. His first thought on seeing this young man was that he should work and gain a position, instead of spending all his time in the churches, and remain in such degrading poverty. But very soon this judgment passed from his mind, and he saw before him a contemplative, favoured by evident signs of celestial intercourse. His exquisite and sweet serenity in the midst of utter destitution shed a heavenly radiance about him, and to the religious-minded proved him beyond all doubt to be a friend of God.

Joseph Locaja, a Jesuit brother, after the suppression of the Society, frequented this church in the morning, and during the day attended the many functions in Rome. Everywhere he saw the poverello. Kneeling behind him one day he overheard the thrilling accents in which he breathed out the prayer *miserere mei*. Locaja was moved to tears. In the streets he tried to enter into conversation, but as he unconsciously showed his respect, Benedict avoided him. It was only by affecting to despise the mendicant that Locaja succeeded in exchanging a few words with him. By dint of watching, he made a study of this wonderful penitent, and was appalled at the severity of his mortification. Locaja feared that, notwithstanding the special graces he received, nature would break down and rebel. Locaja would see him drenched by rain and snow, his feet covered with mud, his legs half bare, frozen and blue with cold, continuing in prayer for hours, even the whole day; his marvellous serenity not in any way disturbed.

The secret was that blessed Benedict thanked God for every opportunity of suffering a temporary discomfort, in exchange for an eternal reward.

Locaja said to him, 'How can you endure this life? Would it not be better to sanctify yourself in a Monastery?'

'If God had so willed,' replied Benedict, 'He would have arranged it.'

Locaja did not understand the full import of this answer, but he admired more than ever the saint's care to follow only the will of God.

A Spanish Jesuit, Don Joseph Ibarra, took special pleasure in giving an alms to this poor man, who was like the *Ecce Homo*.

Abbé Rossi had remarked him at Monte Cavallo, and was not altogether pleased by his singularity. Since then he had seen him constantly at the Forty Hours' Devotion. When Abbé Rossi became Prefect of the Maronite College, he pointed Benedict out to his pupils, 'Look at that poor man, and you will see how a saint prays.'

When alms were offered to him in church, he took no notice. In the street he would express his thanks by a look, a smile, or a graceful inclination of the head more touching than words.

Locaja had got him to accept a pair of shoes to replace those which were broken in every part, and barely held on by string. When Benedict did accept what was offered, it was more to give the donor the merit of doing an act of charity. A few days after, Locaja met him in heavy rain, his feet soaked in the old sandals. 'Why do you not wear the shoes I gave you?' asked Locaja, reproachfully.

'Oh, these suit me very well,' was the peaceful answer.

The other pair had been passed on to the first beggar in need of them. Nothing astonished the poor more than the alms Benedict gave them so liberally.

'How wonderful!' exclaimed a poor woman to whom he gave at the door of Santa Maria dei Monti, 'to see a poor man giving alms to other poor!'

Another heard him refuse an offer of clothes when he was without stockings, and his rags scarcely covered him. 'Look at this man who needs nothing!' she cried, with a kind of awe. 'Oh, blessed one! God alone is sufficient for him.'

Wherever the Forty Hours' Adoration was held, he was a most constant worshipper.

Many persons in Rome began to form a true estimate of his merits. They would be glad to know he was in the same church with them, and regret his absence, if he were elsewhere. Antonio Silvani was one who believed that in Benedict he saw a saint.

Locaja said of him, 'He is not a man, but an angel.'

He was called *the holy poor, one of the Forty Hours.*

Even as other great saints, this holy being, so penitential, so cautious, so delicate of conscience, was not free from assaults of the impure demon. He invoked the Blessed Virgin, he took the discipline, he redoubled his austerity. He refused to take wine; he fasted the whole year. The enemy had to fall back baffled and powerless before the weapons of prayer and penance with which

Benedict broke every shaft aimed against his virtue. The demon, with all his cunning and malice, could not surprise this pure soul into consent to any of his suggestions. Those who knew the Saint's conscience thoroughly and intimately affirm that he died in baptismal innocence.

He suffered interior desolation; the enemy tried to shake his trust and hope, telling him that his name was not written in the Book of Life. To overcome this temptation he constantly repeated an Act of Hope: 'Lord, deign even to my last breath to increase and fortify my hope.'

When at last this severe trial passed away, the Holy Spirit poured into his soul such Divine light and consolation that Benedict's director said he would gladly have become the disciple of his penitent.

It was noticed that the poor man of God never begged; he often refused alms; those he received were given to other poor; he had reduced his own needs to almost nothing. One day someone passing gave him a small coin. Benedict handed it directly to a beggar near. The donor, thinking he did this in contempt, raised his stick and struck Benedict angrily. The Saint bowed his head and went on his way. A rumour of this reached Dominica Brevi. Wishing to learn the truth, the next time she saw him she said: 'A nice thing to be ill-used for the love of God! One gets an alms, and for not keeping it, one gets a beating.'

Benedict only smiled; his face beamed with the joy he had felt in this humiliation. He was liable to insult from those who saw only his miserable garments. On another occasion he was surrounded by ten or twelve idle youths, who amused themselves by jeering, pulling his hair, buffeting him. His calm patience irritated them, but he was undisturbed; he neither resisted nor defended himself. They threw him then from one to the other with such force that he fell; then with shouts of delight they trampled upon him.

A woman passing by was filled with horror and indignation. She called to them: 'Savages! Do you wish to kill him as the Jews did our Lord!'

Other passers-by joined her, and the wretches slunk away, saying: 'Surely we can amuse ourselves with a fool!' The woman who witnessed this scene belonged to an old Venetian family; her name was Maria Clara Donati. She had suffered great reverses of fortune and many afflictions. In Rome she devoted her life to visiting the churches, and was herself assisted by charity. Even ten years afterwards she could not speak of this outrage upon the saint without tears.

As for him, his desire was to be in the eyes of all poor, despicable, and an object of scorn and disgust. To suffer with our Divine Lord, to share His hunger, thirst, exhaustion, His journeys, His watches, His nights of prayer, His homelessness, not having anywhere to lay His head. This was the single aim of blessed Benedict's whole life.

There was nothing weak about him. His soul was strong to the utmost; it was of burning ardour—its constancy a steady flame. From childhood he made his choice: he would follow close in the footsteps of the Divine Model upon Whom his mental gaze was riveted.

To unsurpassed humility he united a will of extraordinary power: his character, with all its gentleness and docility, was resolute as the grave. His delicate, super-sensitive conscience give him no respite from practising the severest mortification from beginning to end of his wonderful life.

As a youth the rebuffs he met with: his failure in the novitiate, the final quenchment of his cherished hope to serve God in the cloister, were enough to cripple the energy and dim the faith of an ordinary mortal. But his faith was vigorous as his soul.

His frame was vigorous too. His head was well-formed, the

brow large, the eye-brows strongly marked and smooth. His neck was poised upon square shoulders; he was of medium height, his limbs were symmetrical, he moved with ease and dignity. His hands were slender and of so fine a shape that a Roman sculptor asked to model them, offering a reward if the poor man would come to his studio. He was astounded to receive a curt refusal as Benedict hid them in his sleeves and walked away.

The French artist Bley was more successful. When meditating a picture of our Lord he chanced to meet the 'poverello' and was forcibly struck by the expression of purity and elevation of mind upon his countenance; with the downcast eyes and features in repose, was a kind of majesty in face and form; which realised the painters ideal. He spoke at once to the poor man, asking to be allowed to paint his likeness.

Without glancing up Benedict refused.

By his accent Bley recognised a fellow-countryman, and pressed him eagerly. Would he come in the service of God and to oblige a compatriot who was occupied on a pious picture? In silence he went, stood like a statue till the sketch was finished, but would receive nothing. 'May all be for the glory of God!' he said, as he passed out.

DISTANT PILGRIMAGES AND FOURTH RETURN TO ROME

About September, 1774, Benedict set forth from Rome again to make a series of pilgrimages across Italy, Switzerland, France, and Germany. He spent whole days in adoration before the Blessed Sacrament in the Holy House of Loretto, whose very walls were so dear to his veneration that he would devoutly kiss them. They were often crowded with the faithful; he would then retire behind a pillar, not to incommode any one, and to avoid distractions. The sacristan, Gaspar Valeri, in minor orders, was much attracted by this singular pilgrim. He noted his unceasing devotion; even when the church doors were closed he leant against the wall with a book in his hand, reading and meditating. Abbé Valeri could not resist questioning him, and began, 'Do you ask alms?'

'I receive them when given,' was the quiet answer.

'But what do you live upon?'

A gentle shrug came this time by way of answer: it expressed that living was a matter of small consequence.

'What is your name?'

'Benedict.'

'Your family name?' No answer. 'Your country?' persisted the questioner.

'France.'

'Your dwelling place?'

'Anywhere.'

'But, seriously, where?'

'Rome.'

'What is your address?'

Benedict's quick sense of humour was touched, he smiled.

'There are many churches in Rome,' continued the Abbé; 'a person can do much good there without being known?'

'True, I can go freely from one church to another.'

'But where do you sleep?'

'Here, on the steps.'

'Do you not know that the cold of this pavement and the draught from the bell-tower may give you your death?'

'It is as God wills. A poor man like me just casts himself down: he ought not to seek a comfortable bed. Besides, I wish to be alone, and to remain in peace.'

Young Valeri was about to be ordained, and had many scruples. During Benedict's stay he confided them to the holy pilgrim and begged for his prayers. While the young Abbé spoke Benedict listened attentively in his usual attitude of prayer; then, raising his eyes to heaven, he replied in firm tones, 'All will be well.'

Abbé Valeri's ordination took place soon afterwards. He believed that his poor friend's prayers won for him entire peace of mind and success in his vocation. His veneration and love for Benedict grew stronger year by year as he had wider opportunities of knowing his sanctity. When first he saw Benedict he had noticed, with surprise, that his books were in Latin, and that he read the Divine Office from a Breviary every day. 'You have been a religious?' he ventured to say. This was in church, so Benedict bowed his head.

Seeing him in the street the same evening Abbé Valeri spoke again on the subject. Benedict said he had been about nine months with the Cistercians.

'Why did you leave them for this abject, miserable life?'

'God so willed it, and we must conform to His will.'

Eagerly Valeri suggested he should stay at Loretto, and be employed in the sacristy, or join the Camaldolese near.

'I will think about it.'

Next day Abbé Valeri awaited his answer.

'God does not wish me to lead that life,' he said simply and firmly.

Père Temple, who had given Benedict the cord of Saint Francis of Assisi, was now French *penitencier* at Loretto. He did not at first recognise the Saint. Later he wrote most important details upon the conferences he had had with him. It was Benedict's rule to place himself under obedience wherever he went to remain for any time. '*Mon Pere*,' said the pilgrim, 'since, by the grace of God and the Blessed Virgin, I am so happy as to be in this sanctuary, I wish to place myself under obedience, and for the present I ask permission, if you think well, to allow me to follow my ordinary rule.'

'But what is your rule?' asked the astonished priest.

'I am content with whatever is offered spontaneously in charity.'

'But if nobody offers?'

'I go to the door of monasteries where soup is distributed.'

'And if there are no such monasteries in the place where you happen to be?'

'There is always something to be found in the street, parings of apples or oranges, cabbage leaves or spoiled fruit, which is sufficient for me.'

'But supposing you do not get any of these remains of food? Would you tempt God, and force Him to do miracles?'

'Oh, then I am not discouraged. I go out into the country, and along the hedges and roads do not fail to find some herbs and roots, enough to satisfy me, with water from the dykes or pools.'

Fr Temple told him in obedience to go with another pilgrim, whom he pointed out, and to eat whatever he gave; and to come to him during the day with his certificates and passports. The priest had some suspicion, and yet a strong feeling with regard to this man, that he could not define. He thought to himself, 'He is either a great saint or a demon.'

He kept a register of the different pilgrims, and after their names generally wrote some remark. After Benedict's he was on the point of writing, 'Suspected of heresy and hypocrisy,' but when he had written the word suspected his pen obeyed an involuntary impulse and wrote... 'of a great contempt for himself.' Fr Temple could not help thinking of this young man, and prayed earnestly for light from Heaven. It came abundantly. Benedict's confessions revealed his soul, and the director was so struck by what he heard that he entered into long spiritual conferences with him. These were a penance to the saint—tears flowed from his eyes when he had to give an answer in any way favourable to himself. Fr Temple looked now upon his penitent as an angel upon earth. These conferences lasted three days, and the French *penitencier* wrote a valuable document on the subject. He 'saw the hand of God was leading this votary of holy poverty in an especial way.' Benedict asked in confession if Fr Temple approved of his joining the Camaldolese, as Abbé Valeri had proposed. Suddenly and involuntarily he felt himself compelled to answer, 'No, my son, God does not call you to that life.'

Directly Benedict found himself noticed 'as something good' he hastened his departure from Loretto. The least show of respect or admiration from others threw him into a state of anguish.

He went on to Faenza, Ravenna, Bologna, Verona, Milan, Turin, visiting all the sanctuaries by the way. It is almost certain that he traversed Alsace-Lorraine and Franche Comté. Wherever he passed, his piety, humility, and wonderful charity to the poor were remarked. He reached Notre Dame des Érmites at Einsiedeln for the first time (he made three journeys to the celebrated shrine) in March, 1775. His memory is well preserved there, and a portrait in coloured glass kept with great veneration in certain families. At Wipkingen the curé invited him to eat at his table, and gave him an old Breviary. He passed through parts of Germany, and in a village of Baden was assailed by a troop of young folk with derision and insult. Then, as always, his serenity was undisturbed.

He came through the gates of Rome for the fourth time on the 7th September, 1775, in time to prepare to gain the Jubilee indulgence granted by Pius VI. If possible, he was even more assiduous in prayer at the Tomb of the Apostles and the numerous sanctuaries near, but Santa Maria dei Monti was his chief resort, where he attended masses, catechisms, and sermons. He spoke little, answering by a movement of his head and was very polite and sensitive. If he saw anyone disliked his proximity, he moved away at once, without appearing to notice their repugnance.

Fr Vides, chaplain of the Spanish chapel, loved to kneel near him at the Forty Hours' Expositions; he felt such a stimulus to his own devotion, and realised the majesty of God more strongly. People began to point Benedict out to each other. 'He is a great

Saint,' said one. 'Depend upon it, we shall hear of him one day.' His humility and devotion are incomprehensible: when I see him in contemplation I think to myself: 'O, happy mortal! Who can tell what wonders you see in the Divine light.' His confessor at this time, Fr Gabrini, a man of great learning, said: 'I declare that although his life is more admirable than imitable, yet all his works must be meritorious and praiseworthy, because he does nothing without the sanction of spiritual directors: he depends upon them in all.' This confessor tested the obedience of his extraordinary penitent in many ways: he did it to assure himself that Benedict was guided by the Will of God, and not by his own inclination.

The result was that Fr Gabrini said: 'I gave up trying to make him change his mode of life when I saw that he was especially assisted by God, who led him by this road into the way of perfection. The complete indifference to contempt and outrages, or rather the satisfaction he took in them, was founded upon perfect humility, upon a desire to suffer for love of Jesus Christ. His sordid dress was part of that desire. I was able to measure the grandeur of his soul and the sublimity of his virtue.'

We now first hear of Zaccarelli, a devout man who used to receive Holy Communion every Saturday in the church of Santa Maria dei Monti, and pass the whole morning there in those days. He admired Benedict, liked to kneel beside him, gave him alms, and tried to enter into conversation when they left the church, receiving very short replies. Zaccarelli was a butcher; his home was close to the church; he and his family became deeply interested in the 'holy poor one' who passed their door so often. It was afterwards in their home that the saint came to die.

WHAT SOME PERSONS SAID OF HIM

In the beginning of 1776 he again left Rome, and was absent nearly the whole year. He crossed the Apennines in the most rigorous season, was back at Assisi and the sanctuary most dear to his heart, Loretto.

Fr Valeri told him not to sleep on the ground near the church, but to go to a country barn, which he did. This priest, as well as Fr Temple, became more impressed by his sanctity. Fr Valeri said to his friends: 'If you survive this poor man, you will hear it said that he died a great saint.'

After a sixth pilgrimage to Loretto he returned to Rome, and remained in Italy till his death, going to Loretto once each year.

When on his way there in 1778 he met a very old man returning. He was a Persian named George Zitli, a convert of thirty years; he had fallen into great poverty, and, like Benedict, spent the greater part of his time in the churches. The old man was much edified by all he heard of Benedict in the different places where he stopped.

Zitli was born at Ispahan, had been governor of Teheran, and treasurer to the state. He had been obliged to leave his country when the kingdom was overthrown, and his own wealth lost. Passing through a hamlet, he heard a woman telling how her child had been cured two days before by a poor young man to whom she had given hospitality in her stable. Hearing the sick child's cries, and seeing her distress, he placed his hand on the child's head, and said to her, 'Take comfort, he will not cry any more.' The boy fell asleep directly, and in the morning he awoke quite well. By the woman's description, Zitli recognised Benedict. They met three months afterwards at Rome. Zitli was astounded that his friend could live in such destitution.

'Ah, fear nothing; I am quite content with my position,' was the happy reply.

The old Persian was so touched by Benedict's virtues that he said to the Capuchins of Piazza Barberini, who befriended him, 'I have travelled over all parts of Europe, and many of Asia. Since my conversion to the Catholic religion I have had the happiness of knowing many great and good men, priests and religious of various orders. Never have I seen anyone practise virtue in the same perfection as Benedict. In examining closely his way of life, and noting the extraordinary joy always upon his countenance, it seems to me that he carries the practice of Christianity to sublime heights.'

Benedict's love of solitude when not in adoration of the Blessed Sacrament was because he never lost the sense of the Divine Presence. Converse with God was his sole occupation, only interrupted when the interest of his neighbour claimed attention. As a child he realised that, 'to be with Jesus is a sweet paradise.' The one science he had striven to learn was how to remain in His company. Benedict's strong spirit had grappled with the truth: 'No man can serve two masters.' By the grace of God he had made an early choice; he did not understand compromise; he took Saint Paul's estimate of the things of the world, and suffered the loss of them all, that he might gain Christ.

His communions were often made at the church of Santa Maria Maggiore. One of the congregation said, 'I have seen him arrive in mid-winter, under a torrent of rain, completely drenched; his garments had to dry on his body, and benumbed as he must have been, he did not seem to feel any discomfort during his prolonged prayers.'

One of his charities was to carry alms every week to a poor hermit who guarded a little chapel built on the spot where Saint Ignatius Loyola and Saint Philip Neri met. He was seen in the most inclement weather, soaked by rain or snow, his bare feet in mud or water, continuing his visits to the sanctuaries, where he remained hours in prayer in perfect serenity and joy. The sight of him, living of the love of God, entirely detached from the world, consoled and encouraged many.

A lady leaving the church at the same time as the *Poor man of the Forty Hours*, said to him, 'Blessed you! Who are so good.' The least word of praise troubled him. Tears filled his clear blue eyes, he lowered his head, then instantly turning his back, he hurried away.

In 1779 he made his usual journey to Loretto. When speaking to Zitli of the Holy House, he said, 'Although, by the permission of God, I came out of the monastery, I hope not to be vanquished by the devil; but rather, with the help of Mary, to crush his head. So I feel a great joy when I visit Loretto, and thank my Lord each year that He lets me come.'

On the return to Rome, Benedict became seriously ill. Saint Martin's Hospital—opened by the directors of the Evangelical work—received twelve poor for the night. Theodore Grimaldi, the custodian, met Benedict, scarcely able to drag himself along, because of the swelling of his legs. Distressed at his state, Grimaldi brought him to Fr Paul Mancini, the Administrator, who knowing his character, gave him a kind welcome. Benedict, feeling that necessity for treatment was an indication of God's will, accepted hospitality. Fr Mancini saw that he took all the remedies prescribed.

No sooner was he able to walk than he said to his benefactor: 'You see, sir, that now I can go with other poor to the Convent doors for my food. I need no longer deprive another patient of what you give me here. But how can I thank you, for without your aid I must have died.'

'Remember me in your prayers,' the priest answered.

'How could I forget you,' said the Saint.

This experience showed him that he should not continue to sleep in the open air as before. Padre Mancini gave leave that he should be admitted every evening to sleep in the hospital. When Benedict wished to start for Loretto he asked Fr Mancini's permission. The priest gave him a letter for the Abbess of Poor Clares at Monte Lupone. He arrived on the morning of Holy Thursday, and despite his extreme fatigue assisted on his knees at the whole office for the day. After the ceremonies he presented the letter.

Opening it, the Abbess read the words, 'I send you the holy poor one, whose life is spent in prayer.' The community came to the grille that they might see a saint.

One sister, noticing his miserable clothes, could not help saying, 'Poor unfortunate!' Up to this Benedict had kept silence. He now said, 'The only unfortunate are those in hell, who have lost God for all eternity, not so the poor of the earth.'

Some questions were asked about his benefactor, Fr Mancini, to which he gave the single response, 'He loves God.'

Dinner was offered; Benedict ate very little. Pressed to take more, he said, 'Today Divine Providence has given me all that is necessary; keep this for other poor.' He left very soon, refusing to take any provision for the next day.

Asked by Fr Mancini, on his return to Rome, if he had brought an answer to his letter, Benedict said he had left quickly. 'The community recommended themselves to my prayers, as if I were something good, whereas I am nothing but a vile sinner.'

At Loretto Fr Valeri found him a lodging with Gaudenzio and Barbara Sori, who kept a small hotel near the church, and readily took in the poor pilgrim. He refused the room they showed him, humble as it was.

'It is too comfortable,' he objected, 'not suitable to the poor. It is enough to have shelter for the night and a few feet of ground to lie upon; let me have a corner below.'

They took him into their kitchen for supper.

'Oh,' he said, 'it is too much charity. Was it not enough to give me a lodging?'

He would only eat some remains, and would have nothing prepared for himself. They offered him linen and clothes; he would only accept what was absolutely necessary, and those very worn. He hid the waistcoat under his old coat with the smiling excuse, 'A poor man must not show his grand clothes.' He ate but once during the day—after leaving the church when the doors were shut for the night. He neither came in nor out of his host's house without their invitation. Gaudenzio and his wife said later that the holy pilgrim had brought the blessing of God under their roof. They were in anxiety and in debt, but after his arrival all went well with their business and their home.

They gave him an invitation for the following year. 'You see,' said Barbara, 'that it is a real pleasure to us to give you hospitality, and we treat you without ceremony, just as a poor man.'

A PRIEST OBSERVES HIM AS AN EXAMPLE

Benedict was back at Rome in June, 1780, to continue his life of prayer and charity. The presence of the Vicar of Jesus Christ was one great reason for his love of Rome—he never heard the Pontiff's name mentioned without bending his head in respect. He asked, and received, Fr Mancini's permission to pass his nights in the hospital: his days were spent entirely in the churches. On Mondays and Thursdays he used to attend the midday Benediction at the Santi Apostoli Church. The sacristan there told him he might serve God equally well and yet take some little care of his health and appearance.

'That is of no use,' said the pilgrim.

At length, in obedience, he consented to change his ragged garment for a dark grey overcoat, given by the sacristan Giansanini, which he wore till the day of his death.

People could not understand how, in his state of bodily weakness, he could remain kneeling for hours motionless as a statue, with the face of an angel. The Passion of our Lord was always present in his mind. His contemplation of the sorrowful mysteries seemed to have made them his own, and people saw him follow the Stations of the Cross with holy awe, as if the Redeemer were actually amongst them in His form.

Another source of wonder was that he was seen in many distant churches on the same day. 'How did he get there?' people asked themselves. Was he already gifted with the speed of the blessed?

In the summer of 1780 he had fever, but would not accept offers of treatment and care.

'Oh, it is not worth your trouble,' he would say; 'divine goodness will provide for my cure.'

At the Forty Hours, one day a priest saw him for hours in adoration on the gospel side of the altar rail. Returning after a long absence the same priest, to his surprise, saw that the mendicant was still there, looking, as he afterwards said, 'like a seraph in the presence of his God. How ashamed ought we priests and Christians to feel who find it sometimes difficult to pass an hour before the King of kings; while this poor man, badly fed, half-clothed, exhausted by mortifications, remains there upon his knees for hours together, motionless.'

After Benediction someone saw him give to a poor woman the alms he had received. The gentleman said to his friends, 'Do you see that man with the exterior of a beggar? Would that my soul might have a place in Heaven at his feet!'

Benedict treated his body with utter scorn, as being a drag upon the spiritual life; yet his vigilance over his senses was never relaxed, and thus he was raised above all human likes and dislikes. One afternoon, on leaving the church of Santa Maria dei Monti, fasting as usual, he passed a cook-shop whence came an appetising odour. He stopped and asked to buy a portion of what was fried. He was known to everyone in that part, and the cook said she would not sell, but would be delighted to give him some. He thanked her for the offer, but instantly walked on, and was seen at a little distance to strike himself on the mouth, as if to rebuke it for daring to be hungry. The incident brought tears to the eyes of a priest who chanced to see it.

During Lent, 1781, Benedict started for Loretto, and Fr Mancini wished to send a pilgrim with him because of his failing health. Benedict asked to go alone, so as 'not to be disturbed in his prayers.' Heavy rains made walking very difficult. Easter passed, and he had not arrived at Loretto. One morning after the octave, Gaudenzio met him as he entered the town, broken with fatigue.

'Come up to my house, Benedict,' was the cordial invitation.

'To the Madonna first; afterwards I will come on to you.'

He spent the rest of the day kneeling in prayer before the altar. When the church was shut he came on. Barbara and her husband asked him to eat and accept a change of clothes in obedience, reminding him of the command of Jesus, 'Eat what is set before you.' Fr Valeri had told him to rely upon his hosts for food and clothing.

One evening Barbara, occupied with customers, had not bid Benedict enter; when at liberty she looked out into the street. There he was, leaning against a wall, quite still, his head bent forward and his arms folded, as usual, over his breast.

'Why do you not come in?' she asked. 'There is no hurry; you must serve your customers. I can wait,' he answered gently.

After fifteen days of adoration in the Holy House he announced his departure for the morrow. Fr Valeri gave him some medals and offered him money.

'What should I do with it? The poor do not carry money,' was his decided negative.

In vain the Soris pressed him to stay longer. He prayed all the morning in the Santa Casa, and at midday took leave of Gaudenzio, who happened to be alone in his house. Benedict would accept nothing but a stick stronger than his own.

HIS LAST PILGRIMAGE TO LORETTO

Step by step Saint Benedict Joseph's life has been traced with minute care, and with ever increasing enthusiasm on the part of those who were charged to collect evidence of his sanctity. It was no secret to the Romans, who spoke of him as the French Saint.

In his contemplation he was lifted far into the unseen, and was admitted to penetrate mysteries of the Holy Trinity only revealed to the pure of heart and the spiritual mind. Someone had once to call his attention to the closing of a church, and said he 'looked as if he had been drawn from a sea of delights to be thrown back upon the stream of earthly pains.'

His extraordinary virtues were as much admired by the poor, his companions in the hospital, as by the enlightened confessors who saw into his soul more intimately. To most his very name was unknown. During the last two years his bodily strength declined visibly, but his spirit was raised into ever loftier regions of contemplation; and the gift of seeing into the consciences of others, as well as that of predicting events, was added to the rest.

'Go, my child, and be reconciled to God; hasten to make a good confession, for your death is very near,' he said one day to a young man he met upon the road.

The young libertine scoffed at the warning, and died suddenly a short time afterwards in his sins.

On another occasion Benedict approached someone passing, and said in his gentle and penetrating voice, 'Dear brother, drive away that thought, it is a temptation of the devil.'

The astonished listener accepted this advice, and at once turned away from the sinful purpose he was meditating.

After his last confession Benedict told his confessor what God had revealed to him concerning the calamities which menaced the world, and France in particular. He looked upon these visions as temptations. He finished always by saying, 'Penance alone will disarm the anger of God.' One day, with indescribable distress and grief, he said he had seen his own funeral, and a crowd of people giving honour to his wretched body.

He left Rome on March 6th to pay a last visit to Loretto, crossed the Apennines in most severe weather, being miserably clad, walking in snow, and reduced by every kind of privation. He appeared at the Sori family's door; they begged him to rest a little by the fire and take food.

'I come straight to you,' he said, 'because I promised to do so last year; but I fear to inconvenience you. I lost my way in the snow; but I want nothing now, except, if you will allow me, to put down my wallet. Then I shall go and salute the Madonna, and will come back to you this evening.'

He followed his usual custom of not leaving the Holy House till the doors were shut.

Barbara set before him a more nourishing dish than usual.

'This,' he said, 'is not food for the poor; it is too rich and delicate.' On Good Friday he took herbs, a little bread and water, instead of the small fish she had prepared for his one meal at night. 'Think of the sufferings of Jesus for us on this day! His food was gall and vinegar; and do you wish me to eat?'

'But if we do not eat,' replied Barbara, 'we shall not be able even to pray.' Then, with swift compunction, she added, 'Jesus suffered so much, and I can bear so little, that I have reason to fear for my salvation.'

'You, you,' Benedict rejoined with emotion, 'I too, I am afraid.'

Yet this man's confessors had the certainty that he had never been guilty of any mortal sin; that he had not lost his baptismal innocence; that he was exempt from wilful venial sin. He was penetrated with the love of God, and had a wonderful knowledge of His majesty and His attributes. He had never failed in any obligation, not even those he had imposed upon himself; yet he accused himself with tears of being a vile sinner, unworthy, ungrateful, because, he said, of his many infidelities to the grace of God.

Benedict was first in the church when the doors were opened; fasting, he followed all the offices for the day with deep emotion, as he meditated upon the ignominies of the Saviour. Before leaving the Basilica he confessed to Fr Almerici, who had several conferences with him on the ensuing days, and marvelled at his humility and abnegation, joined to such elevation of thought. He might have learned theology from the angels, so clear and precise was his insight into things spiritual.

Fr Almerici could not hide the esteem he felt. Like Fr Temple, he would gladly have entered into conversation with Benedict, but as soon as Benedict saw that anyone was inclined to think well of him, he kept out of their way. Fr Almerici asked him how many times he had visited Loretto.

'This is the eleventh.'

'You will come again next year?'

'*Mon Pere*, I am going to my country.'

'But you will come to Loretto on the way?'

Benedict gave a slight negative movement of the head, and repeated: 'I am going to my country… I am going… to my country…'

When Fr Almerici heard of the saintly penitent's death in Holy Week of the following year, he understood that Benedict had spoken of his true country in Heaven, to which he then knew he would be called away. After eight days, he said, he should start for Rome on the morrow.

'You will not fail to return to us next year?' Barbara asked.

He smiled. 'If I do not, we shall meet again in Paradise.'

To Gaudenzio he made the same reply. Gaudenzio gave him a crucifix to replace his own, which was broken. He thanked him in affectionate terms, contrary to his usual custom, which was merely a word or a sign, because of his rule of silence.

We must admire the charity of this husband and wife, in humble circumstances, working hard to support their young family. They had 'brought the harbourless into their house,' clothed and ministered to him for Christ's sake, with simplest faith, and as a matter of course. Fr Valeri had said that the poor pilgrim should be lodged somewhere; they threw open their door to receive him. His rags made no difference to their zeal, and events proved that the Sori family had entertained an angel unawares.

Fr Valeri said to Benedict as the others had done: 'You will come back next year?'

'It will be difficult,' was his reply; 'but if God wills, we shall meet in Paradise.' He would not allow Fr Valeri to go with him as far as Montreale. 'It would attract too much attention for a priest to be seen walking with a wretch like me.'

'I HAVE JUST GIVEN COMMUNION TO A SAINT'

Benedict's whole life was a preparation for death. He now made that his special intention, without giving up any of his other obligations. Fr Gabrini, seeing his penitent advance so swiftly to perfection, ordered him in obedience to seek another confessor, whose time was not so fully occupied as his own in parish work.

Benedict finally chose Fr Marconi, at the Church of Saint Ignatius, and went to him up to the time of his death. He made a last general confession, and his severity towards himself was greater than ever. For some years he had suffered from two tumours on his knees; they enlarged so much that he began to fear lest he should not be able to kneel. He was told that to cure them he must keep to his bed. He chose to suffer rather than interrupt his devotions. Padre Mancini pointed out that as these painful tumours were caused by his kneeling too long, he should stand or be seated during his prayers.

'I could scarcely bring myself to sit. If the Seraphim veil their faces with their wings before God, what should be the attitude of a worm of the earth in presence of this Majesty! I will take your advice and remain longer standing.'

He went to Santa Maria dei Monti as usual; when he was too exhausted to kneel or stand, he would sit for a few moments on a bench; but he spoke no more of his tumours, which became very large before his death.

At the beginning of Lent, 1783, he took severe cold, which left an incessant cough. He was urged to go into a hospital for treatment, and pious Christians wished to take him into their houses. He was grateful, but gave a decided negative; he left himself entirely to God, saying: 'The providence of God never fails. When one thinks,' he would say, 'that we have promised in our Baptism to renounce Satan, his pomps and his works, in order to attach ourselves to Jesus Christ, born in a stable, not having in life where to lay His head, dying nailed to a Cross to redeem us, oh, then, it is too much indulgence for us miserable sinners to sleep upon straw, to eat herbs and roots, and to die upon a pallet.'

On another occasion he said: 'I am nothing in the world, nothing on earth but a useless burden. I ought then to enter into myself, to do penance, to regulate the affairs of my soul, and to die like a Christian. May God deign to grant me this grace!'

In this state of physical exhaustion his communions were more frequent. He had a great devotion to Saint Joseph, his patron; on the 19th March he prayed nearly all day in his chapel at Saint Ignatius. On the 25th he made his communion in the same church. The beauty of his countenance, the radiant air of beatitude when he received the Sacred Host, so impressed the priest who gave him communion that he exclaimed in the sacristy: 'I have just given communion to a saint!'

He still attended the Forty Hours' Exposition in the different churches, dragging himself along with difficulty: he looked like a walking skeleton leaning on his staff. He felt death very near, and spoke of it, but without anxiety. 'We should expect death with courage,' he said; 'ask for it with ardour, receive it with love; because it delivers us from the miseries of this life; it puts an end to our iniquities; it opens to us the Kingdom of God, which we have so often solicited in vain, saying: "Thy Kingdom come."' He was more than ever absorbed in contemplation; vocal prayers and reading occupied him far less than formerly. People now said: 'If we survive we shall see great things after his death.'

In February, 1783, Abbé Anthony Daffine, secretary to Cardinal Achinto, went under the portico of the Santi Apostoli Church; as it was raining, Benedict was within, near the great door. As the Abbé entered he saw the poor man's figure framed in brilliant light, which shone from his head to his feet. The Abbé stopped for the space of a Hail Mary, gazing at what he took at first to be a phenomenon, but the light shone steadily on, brighter round his head.

Sometimes, when Benedict was in adoration before the Blessed Sacrament or at holy Mass, the light in his soul would illumine his face; his head was raised, his eyes fixed on some celestial vision. This unearthly radiance was seen at different places by different persons, who, with awe and admiration, understood that our Lord was drawing the saint into closer union and to ever higher contemplation.

On the 12th April he was at the Church of St Francis de Paul for the Forty Hours; as he left in the evening he was more than usually exhausted. A compassionate person went up to him:

'You are very ill, my poor man?'

'God's will be done,' he gently answered.

'You should not run the risk of falling dead in the street.'

'Ah! What does that matter?' He was often heard to say: 'Call me, my Jesus, that I may see You!'

He confessed for the last time with tears. Fr Marconi told him to make a second communion in preparation for death. On the 4th April he went very early to Santa Maria dei Monti, and heard the first Mass prostrate on the ground. He then went to the Church of St Ignatius to receive communion, as he had been told.

Zitli met him in the street, and was much concerned to see him so ill. Benedict bent his head, saying: 'Pray for me; it may be that I shall not see you again,' which was the case.

To his last hour he remained the poorest of the poor. Faithful to his rule, he was destitute of all things, a beggar, although he never asked an alms. Near the end of his life, when scarcely able to stand, he would stop before shops in silent prayer, his hands crossed over his breast. Other poor had learned to expect his charity, which did not fail. He would wait till a small coin was given, or a refusal made in the customary words, 'Go in peace'.

Then he instantly moved away, his soft voice breathing out the prayer: *In te Domine speravi, non confundar in aeternum.* 'In Thee, O Lord, I have hoped, let me never be confounded.'

On the 15th Fr Mancini, of the hospital, advised him to suspend his devotions and take rest. He could not resolve to interrupt them in Holy Week. He fainted after going out, but nevertheless he reached the Church of St Prassede, where the Forty Hours' Exposition was drawing to a close. Near the church he bought a measure of vinegar.

'What are you doing?' cried the vendor, as he saw Benedict raise it to his lips. 'It will do you harm, it will make you ill.'

'There is One who drank of it before me, and in this week suffered for the love of man far more than I can ever suffer,' answered Benedict, taking it at a draught.

He passed the morning near the holy column of the Flagellation, and in the evening was again at Santa Maria dei Monti. He fainted several times during the day, and came to the hospital for the night more dead than alive.

Contrary to his custom, he asked to go and rest. He sat upon his straw paillaisse—which is all he would have by way of a bed—and leaned his head against the wall—he never would lie down till the others were in bed and the lights put out.

THE SAINT'S ONE DEEP GRIEF IS THE INGRATITUDE OF MEN TOWARDS JESUS CHRIST

Benedict's confessors were certain that only by the power of God could he have held to the life he led, which he believed to be that marked out for him. His constancy was supernatural; his will, with regard to himself, inflexible, steeled against every thought of softening the rigours of his state. He had become meekness and gentleness personified. With regard to others he was subject to every creature for Christ's sake. In obedience, he would sometimes go near a fire in winter for a few moments, or accept an invitation to sit down at table, and taste dishes offered to him. He had a sort of horror of possessing even the most necessary things. Silver seemed to burn his hands; he would often run after the donor to give it back, or pass the money instantly to the nearest beggar. He held all his senses under such control that on his pilgrimages, when passing through most celebrated towns, he would not raise his eyes to look at anything.

Fr Marconi said that his humility was like a deep sea, immeasurable. One of his greatest merits was the care he took to hide his virtues, and the graces with which God favoured him. He hid his origin and condition, wishing to pass as the vilest of men. But the refinement of his face and manner, and his choice of words, betrayed him. In the confessional, and when led to speak on religious subjects, he was fluent and animated. He had a remarkable knowledge of Latin, and loved it as the language of the Church. He knew Scripture thoroughly in Latin; yet as one of the poor, he would assist at catechisms and instructions with the poorest, and with children.

The rosary upon his neck was a sign to scoffers that he was a devout servant of Mary; everywhere he could be recognised by this emblem. His devotion to Jesus in the holy Eucharist was boundless. During the hours that he remained in contemplation—the highest kind of prayer—his face wore an expression so rapt that many believed he actually saw our Lord with his bodily eyes. In church, and at night prayers in the hospital, his voice, so clear and melodious in the litanies of the Blessed Virgin, failed when the last ejaculation to the Blessed Sacrament was said. His emotion was too deep for words: he adored in silence. One profound grief never left his heart—he told Padre Marconi 'it was killing him'. This grief was the ingratitude of men towards the beloved and adored Redeemer. The eighteenth century was pouring out blasphemy, unbelief, bad books, apostasy. Every blow aimed at the Catholic faith pierced Benedict's heart. It was acute anguish to see his God, his Father, his Friend, insulted by men, for whose salvation the Saviour had shed His blood and died an ignominious death—men who were Benedict's brothers, whom he loved for Christ's sake, for whom he prayed. He wished to expiate, to pray and to suffer.

His body was the instrument for penance: cold, heat, storms, damp, hunger, thirst, all discomforts and privations gave him the means of crucifying the flesh.

An addition to his sufferings were the insects in his miserable garments. He could easily have put an end to that trouble, but it was the severest form of mortification he could inflict upon himself; and because it was a scourge, he chose to endure it. Charity caused him to take every care to spare others the disgust this knowledge might give them. He lived apart even from the very poor; but no one who approached him seems to have suffered the least inconvenience. After his death no trace was found, either in his bed at the hospital, or upon that on which he died, or upon his body when prepared for burial. The flesh was like that of a little child.

When he ascended the Scala Santa (Holy Stairs) he went at midday, during the hot hours, when there would be nobody but himself and the custodian.

'THE CROWN OF LIFE'

On Wednesday in Holy Week, April 16th, came the summons he awaited with such eager desire. In the hospital they wished to deter him from going out, for he seemed at the point of death. He managed to reach the Church of Santa Maria dei Monti, his usual resort for morning devotions. There he heard two Masses, and remained absorbed in prayer. At 9 o'clock he felt himself sinking, and in need of air. His uncertain steps bore him to the door, the grey pallor of death being on his face. He sank down on the steps outside the church. Bystanders came with offers of assistance. They wished to take him into hospital; he asked to be left; would they give him a glass of water? This was brought; he lifted his eyes and hands to heaven in thanksgiving, both before and after he drank it, as if he had received the greatest relief. Tears were in the eyes of those who stood near, and who afterwards described the scene.

Zaccarelli was passing; he hurried to the steps, and there saw his poor friend extended. He called him by name: 'Benedict! You are ill; you must have care; let me take you into my house.'

At the sound of a voice he knew, a voice which had always

addressed him with sympathy and tenderness, the pilgrim opened his sunken eyes; they rested on the kind and devout butcher for some moments. Benedict's lips moved once more: 'Yes,' he said very clearly; 'in your house I wish to go.'

With the aid of a neighbour, Zaccarelli raised and carried the 'holy poor one' to his own house in Via Serpentaria. Benedict wished to be laid upon the floor.

Zaccarelli thought fit not to yield to the humble request. He reverentially placed him just as he was upon a bed, and spread a coverlet over the emaciated form, asking Benedict to leave himself to them in obedience. They tried to revive him, but he sank into unconsciousness.

The dying Saint lay in his attitude of prayer, his hands crossed over his breast, as if asleep. Only a slight pulsation of the heart, and from time to time a feeble cough, showed that life was not extinct.

Fr Gabrini says: 'Since he fell upon the steps of Santa Maria dei Monti, Benedict never recovered full consciousness: he could not receive Viaticum because of this state. He had neither oppressions, nor contortions, nor movement; his placidity had quite a different character from lethargy. Everybody present noticed this singularity, which was the reflection of interior peace.'

The Vicar of S. Salvatore gave Extreme Unction; the Fathers of Penitence of St Agatha's Church recited the prayers for the dying.

Zaccarelli's house was filled with assistants, who came to join in the prayers, and to see a saint die.

In the evening, just as the kneeling throng sent up their fervent petition, *Sancta Maria, ora pro nobis*, his face became white as milk, and he ceased to breathe.

The bells of Santa Maria Maggiore at that moment rang out the signal for the Salve Regina, which the Pope had ordered to be said, to invoke Mary's prayers for the wants of the Church.

It seemed as if the Holy Mother of God, whose devout servant he had been through life, had herself deigned to lead him into the realms of the blessed.

Scarcely had his last breath been drawn when troops of children were heard in the streets, calling: 'The Saint is dead! The Saint is dead!' On the morrow all Rome was moved. Every one wished to see the Holy Poor One of the Forty Hours, whom they now called 'the new Saint.'

Zaccarelli had put on him the robe of the White Penitents of our Lady of the Snow, of which Benedict was a member. On Holy Thursday a concourse of people of all classes thronged Zaccarelli's door; by midday a guard of soldiers had to be placed there to keep order in the extraordinary enthusiasm among rich and poor, nobles, priests, soldiers, and artisans. People of the world, who would not have touched him during life, came to kiss his hands and feet. They brought their rosaries and medals so as to have something to keep which had touched his frame. It was not yet cold, and his members retained elasticity; the usual symptoms of death were absent, and a pleasant fragrance was noticed—the odour of sanctity. The very contact and presence of the body awoke feelings of contrition, of piety, of tenderness, in the hearts of those who flocked round it. His name, *Blessed Benedict Joseph Labre*, was now on every tongue, and twenty-four hours before his death nobody knew it. His confessor, Fr Marconi, knew it for the first time when he received from Fr Mancini, Administrator of the Hospital S. Martin, a notice that his penitent was dead. He hastened to Zaccarelli's house, his mind filled by the thought of this poor man suddenly finding himself before the Judgment Seat of God, laden with merits of which he had been totally unconscious!

Fr Marconi knelt to kiss Benedict's hands, and exclaimed: 'Oh, happy penitence, which has carried him on its wings in one flight to glory eternal!' Speaking of him later, he said there was not matter for absolution in his confession, no shadow dimmed the beauty of his soul: it was entirely possessed by God.

The devout Princess Rospigliosi was one of the first to venerate his remains. She had been delighted to claim a fellowship of prayer with the holy poor one of the Forty Hours . One day, outside the Church of Santa Maria dei Monti, she had given him alms, saying to him: 'Pray to God for me.'

Contrary to his custom, he raised his eyes for an instant, then replied with the humble dignity that graced his speech and manner: 'For one another.' It was a reply he sometimes made to those whose love of God was known to him.

One thought was in every mind—that his remains should rest in the Church of Santa Maria dei Monti, where he had spent so many days in prayer. 'The good Virgin wants him near her,' the poor declared.

All Rome was of the same opinion, so a little before sun-down he was borne into the church, according to custom, the face uncovered. The cortège was like a triumphal procession—the 'holy poor one' was known in every church of the eternal city; the air was filled with his praises. His devotion to the Blessed Sacrament, his reverence for the Madonna, his heroic voluntary poverty, his love for the hidden life. 'O happy Benedict! He is in Paradise; he is among the saints. How beautiful he is! How beautiful!' was heard on all sides. The children, as if by inspiration, continued to cry out: 'The Saint is dead.'

The concourse increased every moment. Not only the population of Rome, but the people from the country poured in from all quarters, demanding to see and revere his body. God willed that it should be honoured on earth, not waiting for the resurrection, when it would wear the glorious robe of immortality.

The authorities were obliged to allow the body to remain four days in the church, and the Blessed Sacrament had to be removed to an interior chapel because of the commotion and movement: there was one continual procession. Several striking miracles took place. Persons who were hopeless invalids were immediately cured on kissing his hands. Nine miracles are proved before the burial, five the day following his burial, and before the end of the year more than a hundred. Several miracles also took place in the room where he died.

People who despised him when alive, because of his appearance and way of life, now acknowledged that the man they thought half mad was one of God's elect.

Every one was anxious to get something that had belonged to him. At the hospital, and in Zaccarelli's house, whatever he had touched was put away under lock and key. The people drew out threads from his white habit, and cut off some of his hair; they also covered him with flowers, which were afterwards taken away as relics.

Fr Marconi says: 'I can affirm that I have never seen, that I have never read of anything approaching the enthusiasm. It is impossible to give a just idea of it without being taxed with exaggeration; yet nothing that one can say is sufficient to describe the feeling and the demonstration.'

On Easter-day, April 20th, 1783, Benedict was laid in the vault prepared in the church. The stone upon which he had knelt so often in ecstasy was placed over his remains.

Before burial the crowd was shut out, and the body removed to the sacristy for final and juridical examination by the first medical authorities. There was no sign of alteration, and the members were flexible. Professors Marconi and du Pino drew up a report, which was enclosed in a leaden tube and placed near the body.

Benedict died at the age of thirty-five years and twenty-one days.

In this short sketch it is impossible to record all that is known of the Saint in Rome and in the many different places that he visited. For seventy-seven years his cause proceeded, the papers filling more than thirteen volumes in folio. He was proclaimed Venerable by Pius IX, September 20th, 1859; and Leo XIII, in view of the number of miracles worked by his intercession, placed him in the catalogue of the Saints on the 8th of December, 1881.

Gaudenzio and Barbara Sori were expecting their poor guest as usual for Easter: they had not understood his prediction the year before. On Wednesday in Holy Week they said in the family, 'Benedict will be here before long.'

'He will not come,' said the youngest child, Joseph, not yet six years old. 'Benedict will not come; he is dead.'

The mother, startled at the child's serious manner, asked, 'Who told you so? How do you know?'

'My heart tells me so,' was his answer.

On Thursday the parents remarked, 'He came at this hour last year; we shall see him soon.'

The child repeated very earnestly, 'Benedict is not coming, I tell you; he has gone to Paradise.'

The Saint's rare sayings never failed to make an impression; many have been collected. In the Hospital St Martin, among the poor, they were especially treasured. He introduced there the salutation: 'Praised be Jesus and Mary;' and the answer, 'May they be praised for ever.'

He gladly bore any humiliation, but when the honour of God or the Church was in question, he never failed to show his displeasure without ever losing charity or prudence. One of the inmates said in his presence that small falsehoods were permitted when excusing oneself.

'Lies are never permitted, even to save the whole world; for the offence against God is a greater evil than the loss of the universe.'

One day a poor man came in drunk. Another said, 'It is better he should be drunk than ill.'

'Are you mad?' asked Benedict. 'Do you not know that drunkenness is a sin—illness is not?'

On another occasion he said, 'Should there be only one damned, we should each fear to be that one.'

His constant recollection caused the others to say, 'It would be sufficient if we had in church as much recollection as Benedict has in the street.' He passed all his days in prayer, and at night scarcely took any rest: he prayed while others slept. Often he was heard to breathe out in most touching accents, 'Oh! *bon Dieu.* Oh! good God;' and '*Miserere mei Deus, miserere mei.*' At early morn he was always up and engaged in prayer.

He reproved evil whenever he saw it, in gentle yet most forcible terms.

A compromise between good and evil drew from him the following reproach:

'A man is dressed and adorned like people of the world; he speaks and reasons like pious folk. He assists with devotion at the offices of the Church, and soon afterwards is engrossed in prolonged and absorbing games. He receives at times the Holy Sacrament, but does not shun dissipation and profane assemblies. He avoids what is contrary to modesty and good taste, and he equally avoids that which opposes sensuality. Life is therefore neither vicious nor penitent, but is it Christian and holy? You have not done any harm, you say, in that repast at which you assisted; but does one know what is harm when one has no idea of virtue? When like you, one regards luxury and disorder as a fashionable custom. When like you, one has neither the fear of God nor the love of duty.

'Let us walk faithfully with an upright heart, in truth, in justice, in the way of God's commandments, and in the love of our Lord

Jesus Christ to the end of our days, so as to enjoy afterwards the eternal rewards. The trial is not so long for us under the new Law as for the just under the Old Testament; for the just of the old Law had to sanctify themselves during the period of a long life, and by faith in a future Messiah; but God seems to have shortened our lives so as to give us more quickly the fruit of our Redemption. Surely I come soon. Amen, come Lord Jesus!'

On another occasion he said: 'The default of a good examination of conscience, of a true sorrow, of a firm purpose, this is the cause of so many badly made confessions, and of the ruin of souls.'

Of the sin of detraction he said: 'The tongue is an instrument of damnation to many.'

'Why is the Crucifix in your room? It is there to judge the state of affairs in your house, in your business, in your conscience.'

He loved to cheer the afflicted by his own marvellous faith.

'Confidence in God honours God, and does a sweet violence to His paternal heart in our favour. The Providence of God never fails those who trust in it with confidence.'

Benedict was jealous for the honour of Gods house. 'Whisperings and irreverences in church are faults most displeasing to God; they are a horror to the angels, and they cause great damage to the soul.'

To some ribald youths he said: 'My children, it is not for this that God has created you and preserves you on the earth.'

Very often he was insulted and stoned, but of that he took no heed, except to walk slower and prolong the opportunity.

Many witnesses of his virtues, who noticed also the air of distinction, which his miserable clothes could not disguise, and which, no doubt, was the result of his entirely spiritual life, thought that this extraordinary man was a pious personage who hid himself under rags of poverty so as to remain unknown and occupy himself solely with the things of God.

Benedict left a lasting impression upon the minds of those who saw and spoke with him, despite his outward squalor. Behind that the Saint was visible. Their testimony places him vividly before us, living in the midst of his fellow-men, alone, unique in his utter renouncement of temporal things. His heart always before the Throne of God, and himself—that I, of whom we think so much, self—totally forgotten.

Luxury, and its companion, Unbelief, have as many, if not more, followers in the present century as in the eighteenth.

Let us then invoke the prayers of Saint Benedict Joseph Labre, and keep in our minds his example, whose earthly existence was a victory over the pride of the eyes, and the pride of life, and who passed into eternity triumphant, more than a conqueror, through Jesus Christ.

The feast of Saint Benedict Joseph Labre is kept on April 16th, the day of his death.

Barbara Sori recorded that when the holy pilgrim Benedict left his wallet in her house she wished to see the contents. During his absence all day in the church at Loretto she opened the wallet, and found two or three very old shirts, a Breviary, some books of piety, and a tin box, which held 'divers papers' and certificates of his Easter Communions. After his death he was identified by means of these papers.

PRAYERS

PRAYER

Almighty God, who didst inspire blessed Benedict Joseph with such deep love and gratitude towards the Divine Redeemer, and tender reverence for His Holy Mother, grant that, by the prayers and merits of Thy servant, some spark of his fervour may be kindled in our cold hearts, to move us to pray for the gift of the Divine love.

Help us to practise in our lives his angelic charity, his poverty, patience, and humility. Deign also to teach us how to pray for the conversion of unbelievers and sinners, for the deliverance of the souls in Purgatory, for unity and peace on earth; so that we may all enjoy in Heaven the eternal rewards, through Jesus Christ our Lord. Amen.

A SHORT INVOCATION TO SAINT BENEDICT JOSEPH USED BY PILGRIMS TO AMETTES, THE SAINT'S BIRTHPLACE:

Oh Holy Pilgrim, who for love of our Divine Master renounced all earthly things to lead a life of constant mortification and prayer, obtain for us from God the grace to sanctify our short pilgrimage by practising your virtues. Saint Benedict Joseph, pray for us.

A MORNING PRAYER RECITED EVERY DAY BY SAINT BENEDICT JOSEPH LABRE:

O God, Creator of Heaven and earth, my adorable Saviour, I thank You for the immense love You have shown, not only for me, but for all the world. I love You above everything, and I wish to love You throughout this day, as for every instant of my life. I beg of You to help me to do Your holy Will, and I love You continuously for the unbelievers and sinners. I wish to pray for them all this day, that You may deign to enlighten them and restore them to Your grace. I wish also to gain all the indulgences that I can obtain for the deliverance of the souls in Purgatory. In fine, have pity upon the unbelievers and sinners! Grant me Your love, O my God. Imprint upon my heart the marks of Your cruel Passion. I love You, O my Jesus, and I give You my heart. Holy Virgin, preserve me this day, and every day of my life, from all sin, so that I may not lose the love of my God, my God Whom I wish to love each moment in every day of my life.

'I give you thanks, Holy Virgin, in the name of all the faithful for the great love that you bear them. I give thanks to you, too, for all unbelievers and for all sinners. Help them, assist them, so that they may return to their adorable God. Be the helper of all during this day, and for ever. Amen.

EVENING PRAYER

God of goodness! I ask pardon with all my heart for having offended You. Lord, my God, I would rather die a thousand times than offend You more. My sweet Jesus! I give You my soul, and I thank You for having taken pity on me during this day. I wish to love You always and continually through the night, although I sleep. I place my soul in Your hands. I recommend to You the souls in Purgatory. Enlighten and help those who live in the shades of death, be they unbelievers or sinners. I pray to You for them.

I give thanks every moment, my Divine Jesus, that You have preserved my life in order to love You ever more and more. I wish to repose in Your Holy Grace. And this heart You have given me! Where can I place it better than in Your own? There then I will place it, O my kind Jesus. It is there that I wish to dwell, and to take my rest. Holy Virgin, I thank you for all the benefits you have procured for me. I recommend to you the souls in Purgatory. Although I sleep, I wish to love you, and render thanks for sinners and unbelievers. Help them that they may be restored to the grace of your Divine Son. Finally, I place my soul in your hands, and under your protection, Holy Virgin, I propose to sleep. Amen.

* * *

These outpourings reveal to us much of the simplicity and tenderness of Saint Benedict Labre's character, and the generosity of his heart.

www.ingramcontent.com/pod-product-compliance
Lightning Source LLC
Chambersburg PA
CBHW060403080526
44583CB00012B/448